AND NONE OF IT WAS NONSENSE

THE POWER OF STORYTELLING IN SCHOOL

BETTY ROSEN

Postscript by Harold Rosen

Design by Kathryn Cole
Cover photo by Wayne Sproule
Cover design by Yüksel Hassan

Published in Great Britain 1988
by Mary Glasgow Publications Ltd
Avenue House
131-133 Holland Park Avenue
London W11 4UT

Reprinted 1990

British Library Cataloguing in Publication Data

Rosen, Betty
    And none of it was nonsense.

1. English language—Study and teaching (Secondary)   2. Storytelling
I. Title

420'.7'12   LB1631

ISBN 1-85234-191-2

10 9 8 7 6 5 4 3   Printed in Canada   0 1 2 3 4 5/9

AND NONE
OF IT
WAS NONSENSE

THE POWER OF STORYTELLING
IN SCHOOL

CONTENTS

ACKNOWLEDGEMENTS

I am grateful, first and foremost, to all my ex-pupils from Somerset School, Tottenham, London, and most particularly to classes 4C and 4R (1985-6), so much of whose writings are quoted (with their generous permission) in the pages of this book.

Others offered encouragement during its composition, either throughout or at critical points: Harold Rosen (who additionally suffered from neglect during my prolonged affair with the word processor), Adrian Peetoom, Charlotte Brook, Sue Hasted and Derrick Sharp.

The figurine on the front cover is a Story Teller Doll, beloved in various versions and sizes in the American Southwest. The artist of this particular doll is Dorothy Trujillo, from Cochiti Pueblo, New Mexico, who kindly gave permission for the photograph. My thanks also to Johanna Peetoom, the doll's proud owner.

EDITOR'S NOTE

Ten minutes into my first reading of Betty Rosen's manuscript I felt compelled to begin reading it aloud. I didn't stop until I had read all of "My Story," while four other editors were listening with obvious enjoyment. In fact, several times during the subsequent editing I would stop and simply read aloud to everyone within earshot.

Betty Rosen is a storyteller, and her talent is obvious to anyone who hears her voice, even over transatlantic telephone lines. Which made my task a difficult one: how does one edit a storyteller so that supreme pleasure is available to a reader who cannot hear her voice and only has the text to work with? I hope I have succeeded. But do read parts of it aloud, to yourself and to others, especially pages 1-6.

Betty Rosen teaches English in the United Kingdom, but this book was edited for audiences all over the English-speaking world. At times I had to find more general terms than those of the specific setting in which her work occurred. For grade-level designations throughout the text, I adopted the following convention: the numbers 1-6 designate U.K. secondary school grade levels. For instance, 5 means "fifth form." A number followed by a slash (/) and a capital letter designates a specific class at a specific grade level; for example, 1/U means the class called U at secondary level 1 in Betty's school. For additional information, you will find a brief glossary of terms on pages 173-174.

Finally, I want to express my gratitude for the privilege of publishing this book.

Adrian Peetoom

One

MY STORY

 PRELUDE

I had a favourite book. It was filled with stories and puzzles and bits to colour in. There were just a few glossy pages, one of which portrayed three fairies, delicate with dragonfly wings, two of them tall, elegant wisps and the other rounded and little. My sister said she was the one with the raven hair, my cousin Brenda was the redheaded one and I was the baby fairy wearing no clothes. But I recognized this as a rather silly idea because I had always worn clothes and my father would never have allowed any of us to do otherwise: he didn't even like anyone to see his own bare feet, never mind letting me have a bare . . . anything except face, arms and legs.

The book came in for a good deal of pounding. The edges of the pages had become blotting-paper mushy and curly, while the spine had almost come adrift, making the threads of cotton underneath pickable. I was enormously fond of this book, and it was only on the most irritable of occasions that scribbles appeared on the duller pages in blue crayon; on happier days I would sit alone in my bedroom speaking aloud straight from the neat rows of little black letters where the tales were kept, in imitation of the voices my sister adopted when she mesmerized me with the activities of all the different characters involved — elf and ogre, dragon and princess, wicked stepmother and impoverished youngest son. Sometimes I would put the book aside and speculate as to what these beings' lives were like when they were outside the mesh of the stories on the pages. I spoke bold words to the window pane while making pretend writing in my misty breath on the cold glass, no longer myself but a brave prince or a shiny knight in the midst of some new adventure; I don't remember ever fancying being a limp maiden or anything actually in need of rescue.

But what was most special about this book, making me keep it out of the way of prying eyes and thieving fingers, was not the contents so much as the cover. It was predominantly blue and red, presenting a pair of chubby children looking like the Ladybird boy and girl before the jeans era, who held between them a large book which they pored over with evident delight. On the cover of the book they were looking at were a pair of chubby children looking like the Ladybird boy and girl before the jeans era, who held between them a large book which they pored over with evident delight. On the cover of the book they were looking at were a pair of chubby children . . . and so on, the same pair of children with themselves on the cover doing what they were doing ad infinitum.

A magnifying glass, stronger than the one in the drawer under the pipe rack where my father kept the secret things I played with when he was at work, would reveal many, many more pairs of children reading my book. Of that much I was sure. But even a magnifying glass — or a telescope! — could not reveal all. The endlessness of it was endlessly a source of interest, food for thought. With bitten fingernail I traced the outline of as many books as I could see, and marvelled that an unimaginable number of smaller and smaller books continued beyond my physical and mental reach. It suggested vistas of boys and girls in a big world beyond Wales, beyond Clydach, Swansea Valley, on the other side of Mynydd y Gwir and the Black Mountains, into the England I had once lived in but couldn't remember, where my father said the grass was always green and lush, and farther off still where foreigners lived — Germans, Japs, Frenchmen, Huns and others. Were there quantities of boys and girls who looked like these two?

I wondered if exact duplicates of me existed in places rich and strange. Would an exact copy of me have a sister Pat and a cousin Brenda? Could there be moments when everyone, everywhere locked themselves into picture-book silence simultaneously? If there was another me somewhere else, was she like me only on the outside, like in a picture, or all through? My me was encased inside what I could see when I looked down at myself or in the mirror. I reckoned I was mainly somewhere behind my face. What was on the inside of other people's outsides?

On the cover of my precious book were these two children, smiling, rosy, clean, duplicated forever, never moving, never speaking. Never speaking. If they were to speak, I was sure they would speak *properly*. They wouldn't say, "I'm coming now in a minute" or "by year" for "here" or "twp" for "stupid," or put a "there's" in front when something was ". . . nice!" or ". . . nasty!" — all of which, and more, my father said were Welsh and wrong and therefore forbidden to one who had to learn to speak *properly*.

Words were dangerous things. There was one day when we were allowed to keep the wireless on after my father came into the room because Toy-Town-by-Ess-Gee-Hume-Bee-Man was on Children's Hour. One of the voices in the radio said something about ruddy cheeks. Ruddy! There we were at the tea table, in front of us a plate of neatly sliced bread and butter, a dish of strawberry jam (my father said the seeds were little splinters of wood and the jam was turnip), floral plates, cups and saucers, a silver spoon in the sugar, the knitted pink tea-cosy tightly in place, a stand with fairy cakes covering the skirts of the embroidered crinoline lady and her trug of yellow roses on the tablecloth — and somebody on the wireless said the word *ruddy!* I was the one, not Pat, whose bottled mirth and horror exploded first, and my father identified the source of our misbehaviour immediately and precisely. He was far from pleased.

Once we had an evacuee, an orphan with a harelip, called Walter Edward Cyril Mitchell, who taught me to say "I chased a bug around a tree" fast over and over, which I duly did outside the back door beside the earthy smells of the privet hedge flowers. My father came hugely out of the house, dragged Walter indoors and beat him for what seemed to be a long time. It was hard to feel sorry for someone as ugly as Walter, but listening to him was nastier than hearing my sister holler when she got slapped or when the pretty cane shaped like a skinny walking stick was "taken across" her calves.

The boy who repeated himself forever on the front of the book wasn't a bit like Walter Edward Cyril Mitchell. He wouldn't have had awful names like that either. These two were probably called Janet and John. Janet looked a bit like my friend Linda Paul, who had been to my house and I'd been to hers, even though to get there you had to walk about a mile down to the village and then up the Swansea Valley road to Trebanos, where trees and big houses escaped from smutty old Clydach with its Mond nickel works. Both the girl on the cover and Linda Paul had short black silky hair, neat like a cap, and dark eyes. When Linda took me into her house, her mother was making bread in a big, warm kitchen, shiny-topped loaves made like plaits. She stared hard and smiled at me all the time and gave me a big hot knobble off the end of one of the loaves, which I chewed while I tried to answer all the questions she asked about my family. She was a large mother. She enveloped me in friendly curiosity while Linda stood quiet beside me as she usually did. The kitchen was so big, but warm and cosy too. I could see through the door into their living room, right across the carpeted space to a dark sideboard on which stood a big fan-shaped candleholder with one, two . . . eight candles in it. Imagine when there was a power cut! We'd had a power cut not long before, and my mother had taken ages to stick the candles on the cracked, odd saucers she kept for such occasions.

Linda seemed as good at home as she was at school, doing just what her mother asked and being so sweet to her plump little brother. I liked her very much. In the school playground she never got cross, not even when others were really spiteful to her — not that she could have done much, because she was very small. I was tall for my age, so I fought anyone who called her a mochyn or a jew, while she cried quietly somewhere behind me. A mochyn was a pig, but what kind of creature was a jew? Everyone was a dirty mochyn sometime or another, but they said "jew" only to Linda. My father would know what it meant (unless it was Welsh) because he always knew, but it might be a word I shouldn't use, so I wouldn't ask. Sometimes they called me a snob because (they said) I talked posh, but I couldn't hear my voice sounding any different from theirs; it seemed a strange, unwarranted accusation which made me thoughtful rather than angry.

Alone in my bedroom I would ponder such things aloud while my finger traced infinity on the cover of my favourite story book. And the boy and girl on my knee passed my secrets on and on down the everlasting tunnel of their existences.

A day came, however, when this area of peace and privacy became public in terrible fashion. It had to do with school, as unpleasant things tended to do. It was a day when some kind of confusion attended the grownups' normal routine. The room partition was pulled back, children from other classes appeared and sat amongst us, and Miss Chilcott (our teacher, tall as a crane, as cold as her name, twin-setted and pearl-necklaced) was joined by Miss Smale. They consulted with each other for what seemed ages up front, presumably over what they were going to do with us.

I waited. We all waited. I roved my eyes around, bored. Gladys Parkhouse had the birthmark side of her face away from me, and she looked quite pretty. I wondered yet again if a birthmark hurt and whether she'd swap her mass of corkscrew ringlets for an unbirthmarked face if she could be given a magic wish. I'd have to ask her. I didn't think she'd know whether the birthmark went right the way through to where Gladys Parkhouse was on the inside, so it probably wouldn't be worth asking about that.

Clive Davies, dirty and long-leggedy, lounged all over his desk as usual, smelling of scarlet fever, headbugs and rabbit hutch. They all smelt like that if they came from the Flats, which I must never, never go near. Dolly Thomas came from there. Sometimes she would go to sleep with her head on the desk, and Miss Chilcott let her. I tried it once when we were doing Welsh, which my father said he'd be down to "look into," but he must have forgotten about it because I had been struggling through "Y mae ceffyl yn y cae" when I gave up and pretended to go to sleep — but Miss Chilcott woke me up straight away. Perhaps the Dolly Thomas on the inside was clever but always too tired to show it, so she seemed twp to us. Perhaps she was like Cinderella and just needed some new clothes to prove it. Someone said she didn't wear any knickers, so I once got down on my hands and knees in the classroom at the beginning of playtime and tried to look up her shapeless skirt, but I didn't find out because her skirt was so raggedy, long and dark I couldn't see anything and because Miss Chilcott got hold of me in the middle of my endeavours and gave me a good slapping for being rude — which I wasn't. Dolly Thomas's skin was the colour of the uncooked leftover pastry my mother gave me to make into little men, which were cooked with the pies and given to my father with his supper when I was in bed.

Suddenly there was a look of purpose upon our teachers and they were shooshing us into silence. Miss Smale said we would have a story. There's lovely! We didn't have stories anything like often enough at school. It was lucky for me I had a story every night, squashed in and cuddled up beside my mother in her armchair with Peter Rabbit or Little Black Sambo or Aladdin. A story! This would keep even Dolly Thomas awake. I didn't think her mother would read stories to her in front of the fire like mine did — some people said she didn't have a mother but only a big sister whose clothes would be passed on to Dolly, which was why they were so big; others said her mother went out at nights walking about between the bus station and the market in Swansea, but that didn't seem likely because the market stall-holders started packing up at about five o'clock and everything closed down.

I had a sudden wild moment of daring fantasy as our teachers sorted through a book at the front: what if I let Dolly Thomas come home with me — bugs and all — so my mother could tell her a story? The notion of Dolly Thomas setting foot inside our back door was so unlikely that the thought was killed dead the moment it arose. Even my mother, who was always telling people how she loved all children, would have been horrified. But my father! He wouldn't even allow Monica Murphey in because she always had a runny nose, so ever after she simply pressed it, and its pale-green elastic jelly, against the bars of our gate, watching longingly as I left her to make her way farther up the street to her house. That was the one thing which made me wonder if my father really was always right; I couldn't imagine he was anything but always right, and yet when he banned Monica Murphey because of a dirty nose — which was, after all, on the outside of her face, not actually where the real Monica Murphey was — it seemed as though something had been missed out from my father's calculations somehow . . . if that were possible.

Well, we'd all have a story today. Our teachers were ready at last and Miss Smale was about to start. "Once upon a time, in a deep forest . . ." But I heard no more of that story. Miss Smale lifted the book from which she was reading so that the cover became visible to us. The cover was predominantly blue and red. On it was a picture of two children, a boy and a girl, looking like the Ladybird children, who held between them . . . It was not possible. But there it really was in Miss Smale's podgy hands: my favourite book. My mind, my thoughts, my secrets seemed to have ballooned together and burst into shapeless fragments. My favourite possession! How could such a gross intrusion have occurred? Miss Smale was too fat to have hidden in my bedroom. Somebody smaller must have got through the window and secreted herself (or himself! unthinkable! what would my father say?) under the bed. But when and for how long? Had the thief observed me pretending to be my reading sister or talking to myself at the window or exploring my private thoughts? Then she — someone — had stolen my book and a piece of my secret self.

My first tears were soundless, but as my incredulity turned to hysterical outrage, the noises I tried in vain to stifle increased well beyond the level that teachers can ignore. Everyone looked at me in amazement as they cried out superfluous appeals to our teacher on my behalf. I don't think I saw them. I certainly don't remember making the trip from my desk to the front of the class where in a blur I saw both those women bending over my weepings, howlings and hiccuppings, badgering me for the explanation of my startling piece of class disruption. I didn't want them to touch me, these thieves. I could only wail, my eyes screwed up but fixed upon what was lying on the teacher's desk while all other eyes were fixed on me. Miss Smale and Miss Chilcott cajoled, sighed, blotted my wet cheeks and tried to put their arms round me, but I shoved them off, the crooks, because I didn't want them between me and my book. "What's the matter, Betty? What's the matter?" They asked the same question over and over.

Finally, my finger pointing hard, I hurled the words at them: "That's my book!"

This no doubt cleared the air for them, but not for me. I could neither believe nor understand them when they talked to me about publishers and piles of books in bookshops and lots of other books being like mine. Nor could I understand why, after what I had told them, they wouldn't let me take my book home. But most remarkable of all was that later on when I went into my bedroom it had been put back exactly where I had left it. During the weeks that followed I lost interest in it — well, the goodie-goodies on the cover — and took up with a fat volume of Aesop's fables, lots of which I found I could read properly all by myself right to the very end, where there was always a moral to every story.

■ FORTY YEARS AFTER

Those events took place over forty years ago, forty years filled with stories.

There were those my mother told me about her "then" years: about my grandfather getting a job in a brass foundry when he stopped being a lamplighter; about games played with her eight brothers and sisters, hoops, whips and tops, fivestones and dancing round the maypole; about being afraid in the magic lantern show lest the world would end and she would be sent straight to hell because she wasn't in the chapel; about people putting straw down over the street cobbles to muffle the sound of horse-drawn carts, just as the children muffled their sounds of play because of the girl in a bedroom above who was dying of tuberculosis — it was always quiet, she said, when someone was dying.

There were the make-believe stories she sometimes told me, seated on my bed before she shook my pillow, tucked me in and kissed me goodnight. There were also those she read every evening, just as I said, stories of many kinds including some, like *Little Black Sambo*, that I am now rather ashamed I enjoyed. We got through all the *Rupert Bear* books and, well beyond the age when I could read for myself, she read a chapter or two of whole novels, serialized evening by evening. I remember best the wild adventure of *Treasure Island* and a Victorian tear-jerker called *Little Meg's Children*, who were brave and virtuous little orphans.

I heard stories at school, too, at least until I began taking the bus every day eight miles up the Swansea Valley to Ystalyfera Grammar school where there were no stories at all, except for the gossipy sort of tales I'd avidly digested in the playground of Clydach Junior.

Hundreds of stories I read for myself, in my bedroom mostly, with pure delight; some, by Edgar Allan Poe and his ilk, with awful fascination leading into terrible nightmares.

Stories from my own far-off days have coiled themselves into the weave of tales acquired ever since. In more recent years I have come across and pursued stories from my pupils, a process that escalated when I began encountering children who brought with them, via parents and grandparents, stories from more distant places — the Caribbean, Asia, Africa — and real-life narrations off boats carrying Vietnamese refugees or from territories disputed by Greek and Turkish Cypriots.

My ears opened to adult tellers of tales as well. Paul Keenes-Douglas (Tim-Tim) I first heard on a borrowed LP, his Trinidadian humour and dialogue intriguing to me but causing a sensation among my first group of London West Indian fifteen-year-olds, which proved a breakthrough in English lessons. The broadcaster and performer Alex Pascall provided my introduction to dozens of Anansi stories. And so on. Visits to Canada and Australia threw up still more tales, and I would return with books and tapes full of them. My most precious is, perhaps, a tape of Sylvia, a Cree Indian woman from Alberta who learned harshly and painfully to be ashamed of her family culture while she was a little girl at school — just about the time I was complaining about having to learn Welsh. Her story had a happy ending: the same education system took her up again, by which time she had relearned the riches of her heritage while rearing eleven children. She acquired a university degree and became a teacher armed with many a traditional story to aid her in her commitment, which was to ensure that Cree children would not reject the old ways of their own people. Her tale is amazing and moving.

When I began to involve myself in storytelling at my place of work, it was not, therefore, to take up something totally new, but to put to professional use what had been revolving in my head for as long as I could remember; so long, and so much of it, that I hardly know how to unravel the parts and identify the strands that influenced me most. Perhaps I don't need to: most teachers will have a similar story-store and can get down to the telling business without knowing why this tale is remembered and that one not, just as I did.

To believe in the *value* of doing so is another matter, however. Introducing that side of things here means looking at some other very different features and landmarks on the road from the then of "my story" to the here and now of this book. To use storytelling as a major way of teaching and learning there must be, above all else, the certainty that children (all children, all people) have the capacity to transform and create out of what they receive. Most English teachers — well, *my* kind of English teachers, which is an enormous number! — assume this up to a point, whenever they try to inspire children to write after reading poetry, stories, plays and novels with them, even if there is a stronger faith in the power of the literature than in the power of the pupils. But to close the books, look at the kids, tell them a story from scratch, then ask them to tell that story back again (which is what this book is about) puts the whole process into a new dimension. It presupposes an enormous confidence in people to know that something new and good will come from every child.

I was a long way from that kind of confidence in my primary school days. It was observable in Miss Chilcott's classroom that a few were clever and therefore worthy, most were ordinary and some were twp. Everyone knew that Dolly and Clive hadn't a hope of going to grammar school. Even when I was sent to the top class, where I spent my last few weeks at that school so I would have the opportunity to take the scholarship exam (grammar school entrance) a year early, I saw Clives and Dollies and plenty more who simply were not good enough. My father, the one who *knew*, the one who was *always right*, would have confirmed this view of people had I been looking for confirmation of it. For one thing, these children (my friends) were nearly all Welsh and therefore by nature inferior; the English were the salt of the earth, you see, and Britannia ruled not only the waves but most foreign countries as well. For another, most of them had fathers who were not metallurgists with laboratories of their own full of ammonia smells; they couldn't stir the contents of five test tubes by holding them between the fingers of one hand and shiggling them round all at the same time without spilling a drop; they didn't heat up their morning coffee in a glass beaker over a Bunsen burner; they never had a human lung, heavy with coal dust and silicosis, to analyse; they did not know the exact spot to kick the polarograph to make it go if it broke down. Oh, no! Their fathers were *labourers* — down the mines or in the factory where my father worked, but nowhere near my father's lab, of course. This meant they didn't — and most certainly shouldn't! — possess a car like we did, have holidays in glorious Devon or own untouchable "capital" (whatever that was). Such people bred children who did not speak correctly and who would fetch up at the rough senior school at the end of our road, taking their runny noses with them.

I suppose I should have taken to school with me the gospel according to my father, but for some reason that will ever be unfathomable, I didn't. I can't claim to have rejected it, and certainly would not have dared to question it. It was simply there; I neither felt it inside me nor acted upon it. I vividly recollect the worst thing he ever said to me — at me — when, years on, I told him I'd been allowed by an organization I was involved with at the time to travel in a first-class railway compartment: "Better that way. At least you won't find a nigger sitting next to you." Strange though it may seem, I still loved my father. He loved me, didn't he? At the bench where he was working when he heard Walter teaching me to swear, he would plane a bit of wood called a shim-sham-for-meddlers which turned into a doll's cot or a little desk and stool by Christmas morning; and he took us to the bays of the Gower coast every fine Sunday, where he would climb the rocks with me and help to catch crabs. Perhaps I loved him also because in his dealings with adults, if not with Monica Murphey and poor little Walter, he didn't act on his own gospel either — it was really all talk within the castle of an Englishman's home where he spent most of his non-metallurgical hours: he didn't drink or go out with mates like other dads. Lots of people are like my father and they don't seem to do much harm in the world except, perhaps, to public opinion.

It was a different gospel that actually led me to have faith enough to tell children stories. The seeds of it were there in Miss Chilcott's classroom as I wondered what lay behind hatchet faces like hers, and faces that were birthmarked or harelipped or drained of healthy colour. Even fantasy folk in stories I reckoned had lives beyond what I was told about. Teaching has provided the answers to much speculation about the real nature of people. There are no duplicates of individuals anywhere in the world, which is indeed vast, and each one is miraculously unique. To winkle out that uniqueness has been a perpetual task in my job, and in doing it I have found ample cause for confidence in people. Perhaps teaching is about seeing behind this one's obscenities and that one's silence.

I didn't actually begin to learn about the quality inside ordinary people until some time after I had decided, much to my father's disapproval, to take up teaching as a career. I think he had visions of me as a high-powered secretary to a Member of Parliament, a Tory, of course, and preferably a

member of the Cabinet. The last thing he wanted was that I should do what
he said was every Welsh father's ambition for his offspring — to become a
teacher. It took some time for me to pluck up the courage to admit that I
intended to train for work in schools like the one up the road, then a senior,
now a modern secondary school. That caused one of the rare rows I ever
had with him. If you don't question, you have no rows.

It was during my life as student teacher that I witnessed the lesson
that had the most profound influence upon my future career. I was on
teaching practice in a London comprehensive school, the kind of school
where children ages roughly eleven to sixteen and from all social and
ability levels mix together. At times they are "streamed" into ability
groupings, and Mr. Rees's class, 4/R, was second "stream" from the bottom
of eight. Mr. Rees later rose right out of schoolteaching on to greater
academic heights. To a little mouse student in a foreign land of cockney
teenagers, he was distant and eminent enough then, simply by dint of being
an experienced teacher, a Head of English (ready to take on the rough and
tumble of bottom groups down the school as well as the literary elite in 6)
and, at around forty, a member of the older generation. But to the lesson.

I was trying to look as though I wasn't there — which as far as the
pupils were concerned was true — when Mr. Rees filled the doorway,
purposefully. The room immediately grew smaller. 4/R remained noisy,
even though their attention was instantly focused upon their teacher; it
was clear they were ready for good things to come. The topic was "neighbours." In no time the children proved to be as articulate as professional
raconteurs, gleaming with enthusiasm. Could this be the same group of
boys and girls I'd tried to work with the day before, having selected a
passage for comprehension especially for them about the craft of thatching
houses in rural England? The same people who had squirmed, grumbled and
scowled when I failed to understand them because they spoke of *biles*
("Biles! Biles, miss!") instead of *bales* of straw, then nearly rioted when, with
what appeared to them to be mocking laughter, I pompously explained why
I had misunderstood?

Today's topic they found rivetting, and so did I as a listener: I have
never heard, before or since, such a half hour's amazing medley of character
sketches and hilarious encounters. We had only one pair of neighbours, Mr.
and Mrs. Leopold. He worked in some main office somewhere but, though
English too and white-collared, had put one or other foot wrong so that
neighbourly estrangement had occurred, and that was that. These children
of 4/R made me feel deprived. They spoke — and soon afterwards wrote
brilliantly — of a community life unknown to my family. That morning I
discovered that to see behind the faces meant opening oneself up to other
people's life stories — which were as valuable as any literature I might
bring to the classroom. More, these stories themselves often became
literature.

■ THE SETTING

Between then and now my teaching has been about what Mr. Rees's class taught me, in lots of different educational establishments and with folk from eight years old to one of over eighty in an evening class. The principles always remained the same. I'd learned to love literature and I wanted to spread it amongst those I suspected were deprived of it — the Dolly Thomases and Clive Davises. There was something extraordinarily unfair about their lot, as I had been aware for a long time, even as far back as the events of "my story." I would provide literary balm to their troubled spirits, much as well-dressed ladies provided soup and Bibles in the London East End of my husband's childhood. I still believe in *providing* — that's why I always carry to school in my head a stock of stories to tell. But as I had first learned from Mr. Rees's class, *the first resource of the classroom was not what I brought but what was brought by the pupils.*

I was not fully prepared for what I met and learned when in 1981 I got a job at a comprehensive school for boys in Tottenham, north London. My title was Head of the Communications Faculty, and I was to be responsible for English Language and Literature, Modern Languages, Drama, Music, English as a Second Language and Remedial Education.

The school had a bad reputation. But there was a fair amount of make-believe in the stories which hung about, and it took me quite a long time to sift out the truths from the paranoic fantasies. With regard to the faculty, hearsay horror bombarded my ears on a massive scale. From the accounts I was given, there was a coven of witches, demons and Simple Simons waiting in the wings for my arrival. Fortunately, hours of talk with as many people as possible during my first few weeks allowed me to make very different judgements for myself about the nature and skills of my new colleagues.

The pupil population consisted of roughly seven hundred and fifty boys, ages twelve and up. They lived on and around the Broadwater Farm Estate, the neighbourhood where, in the autumn of 1985, serious rioting took place. They represented a wide ethnic mix (mainly Afro-Caribbean, Asian, Greek/Turkish Cypriot) and brought to school over twenty different mother tongues. The atmosphere was not overtly violent, though fights, occasionally serious, did occur. More significant was a macho, brashly abrasive attitude, particularly evident in the kind of repartee that could be heard outside the classrooms. Competition seemed to matter more than co-operation.

Statistics and other information made clear that the school had to accommodate more than its fair share of pupils expelled from neighbouring secondary schools, and that there were many with emotional as well as learning problems — insofar as the two can be separated. There were relatively few pupils of the conventional academic type and yet those were the ones who, it seemed to me, were prized at the expense of the majority. The school boasted that it had "a strong science tradition," which in fact meant that an occasional "high flyer" reached Oxford or Cambridge, perhaps every three or four years. As for the others, assumptions about their lack of potential virtually dictated mediocrity, at best, and often actual failure in the classroom. Moreover, there was little or no acknowledgement anywhere in the curriculum of the pupils' ethnic or linguistic origins. That's what I saw in 1981, on my arrival.

This book does not expatiate upon my role as head of faculty, nor on the splendid work of my colleagues — what followed after 1981 was not total unmitigated success by any means. It simply tells the story of the changes that flowed from an "accident" of Friday afternoons.

For the last lesson on Friday afternoons, normal timetable activities ceased for all 1's and 2's in favour of "leisure pursuits." Groups of about twenty boys would go sailing, play guitars, hoist garden forks, pull out mats for yoga, etc. My slot was with the 2's, a time for story *telling* as distinct from reading. I now know that those sessions brought together — in more powerful and unique ways than I could ever have anticipated — my love for stories and my faith in the power of children. This book describes how, over the next five years, fundamental changes for the better were made by and with the very people I had been warned against.

There was a good deal to be done. First and foremost, the culture of the pupils — indispensable in the learning process — had to be acknowledged. The tacit or overt assumption that these boys were of low quality had to be proved wrong — because it *was* wrong.

I believe the kind of work described here provides evidence enough of the high potential of children who are multi-ethnic, multi-lingual and inner-city, whatever the city — Glasgow, Toronto, New York, Los Angeles, Sydney. But I had to provide the educational establishment with proof of the success of this kind of work, briefer than a book's length and couched in statistical terms. Here it is: In July 1981, out of approximately one hundred and thirty boys who took the school's final examinations, eight achieved a secondary proficiency level pass in English language. In July 1986, the school was much smaller, but out of seventy-one boys, twenty-one achieved that "O" level pass! By then I also knew that I would never find pupils more worthwhile in any classroom, if I were to teach in a hundred different locations.

Two

FRIDAY AFTERNOON STORY TIME

Each week I prepared a story, usually a fantasy, for my current story group (who would spend half of one school term with me) to tell during the last half of the eighty-minute session. But often it couldn't be fitted in: the boys themselves were full of stories, mostly directly from their everyday lives. Some had been picked up from friends, some from their infant or primary teachers' story corners and, best of all, some from granny on their last visit to Trinidad or Jamaica. Stories from real life had always been part of my classroom workaday world, so I had many a good question up my sleeve: "Has anyone got a scar? How did you get it?" or "What was the best present you ever got?" or "Were you ever scared in the middle of the night?" or Labov's "Did you ever think you were about to die?" Such questions elicit story upon story, stories within stories and stories which beget stories in others. No one is left out, because each child is subject to the narrative of his own living.

Once — I don't quite know what led me to do it — I taped some of the children's stories. Here is a taste:

Me: Okay, Kevin, you come and tell your story. And then we'll hear Wesley's story.

Kevin: A long, long time ago when my mum and all her sisters and brothers were little there was a spirit and it's called the banshee and it calls somebody's name and it's something like four days, four weeks, four months and four years later that person dies whoever she cries the name of. And one day my mum and my Auntie Marion and a couple of my uncles and my Auntie Bernie were going down this hill near Clough's, this little pub shop, and suddenly my mum was shocked. She just stood still in shock. And my Auntie she went up to her and they seen the banshee — that's what my mum told me — and she was calling out someone, I forget whose name but she was calling out someone and the week, four weeks later my Auntie Bernie broke her leg, my Auntie Marion fell into a beehive — she was running round the beehive and she fell into it. She could have died and my grandad died four weeks after as well and my mum broke her arm. And there was something else. There was something else. Oh yes. My uncle Nick. He was — I think he was eleven and he was smoking in the stacks of hay and he made a hole in it, he burnt it down. The ash fell off and he just left it and it burnt down.

Me: Goodness. And all because of the banshee, you reckon. Oh, Stuart. All right then. Thanks, Kevin.

Stuart: I don't believe it myself but I had an old friend. He's an adult and he used to work at my mum's old work and his name was Alf, right, and he told me this story. When he was young he used to live on this farm and he had lots of horses and one day one of these horses had a child, a little foal and the next night the foal died. So Alf went — that's what I call him, Alf — Alf went to bed and he heard this scratching noise down there on the farm, right, so he woke up his brother who was a bit older than him and his brother put on his slippers and his gown and so did he and they went downstairs and as they walked towards the shed where the foal died it was getting louder and louder, right, and when they got into the shed there in the corner they saw the white figure of a little foal scratching away at the corner of the shed.

Me: Good gracious. Did it last long?

Stuart: And then, then he just said that the horse noticed them and he went, he disappeared — he just disappeared. And when they woke up next morning they weren't sure if it was true or not but when they went into the shed there was a hole in the shed.

Me: A hole in the shed?

Stuart: Yes, you know, a hole in the earth in the corner of the shed where they'd seen him scratching, pawing the ground by the corner.

Me: Well thanks, Stuart. There are actually quite a lot of stories about phantom horses. And phantom dogs. Wesley, have you got a story? Come on then, let's hear it.

Wesley: My nan goes and visits my great grandad. She's his daughter and one day when she was coming back from visiting him she was coming back through Bruce Castle Park — she'd been out for a walk with him that night but she was coming back on her own and this was about twelve o'clock. And as she got up to the building in Bruce Castle Park she saw this white figure of a lady. She saw her, like, running and waving her hands as though she was in danger and my nan began to run too, to see what was wrong, and she watched and saw the lady go into the castle. And she stared a bit longer and then she saw this lady ghost come out with a man and my nan got scared and she ran off. My nan reckoned it was that bloke who died in there — coz it's been in the paper. It's been in the paper that a lot of people's seen it.

At this point there were lots of bellowed voices, mainly in confirmation of the strange goings on just up the road from the Broadwater Farm Estate in Bruce Castle Park. Then even more stories poured out. And they were lapped up as the boys relished what was on offer.

Occasionally a group would throw up a really talented performer capable of holding everyone's breath; it was never necessary, though, for a boy to be exceptional in the tellings for every listener to hold his tongue. It made no difference if the tale was secondhand as long as it was not told as such: the idea was to "revision" it so it became, for the moment, the exclusive creation of the teller.

■ YASMIN

I usually told my own stories in one uninterrupted monologue. Very occasionally I would pause in a storytelling and let the boys hazard their own ending, after which I would give them my prepared one (which was not, I assured them, the "proper" ending, as there was never any such thing!). One such story was about the unhappy bride of Lord Lovell, a tale that had terrified and intrigued me during my childhood days. I had heard it many times, not told but sung by my mother. Even now, if I concentrate, snatches of her voice will come into my head accompanied by the whirr of the Hoover (which "beats as it sweeps as it cleans" and one day, when my big sister was in a particularly spiteful mood while engaged in the compulsory housework, she would, I was sure, ram it right over my toes and I would certainly disappear — phloooomph! — up into its dusty inside forever!), or by the clatter of pans in the kitchen, or best of all by her instinctive fingers on the piano (which read *Koblenz — Maker to the Emperor of Germany* in gold letters, which was a big lie according to my sister, who told me that my father had stuck the letters on to make the piano look posh).

This is what she sang:

THE MISTLETOE BOUGH

The mistletoe hung in the castle hall,
The holly branch shone on the old oak wall;
And the baron's retainers were blithe and gay,
And keeping their Christmas holiday.
The baron beheld with a father's pride
His beautiful child, young Lovell's bride;
While she with her bright eyes seemed to be
The star of the goodly company.

"I'm weary of dancing now," she cried.
"Here tarry a moment — I'll hide! I'll hide!

And, Lovell, be sure you're the first to trace
The clue to my secret hiding place."
Away she ran — and her friends began
Each tower to search and each nook to scan;
And Lovell cried, "Oh, where dost thou hide?
I'm lonesome without thee, my own dear bride."
They sought her that night; they sought her next day
And they sought her in vain when a week passed away!
In the highest, the lowest, the loneliest spot
Young Lovell sought wildly, but found her not.
And years flew by, and their grief at last
Was told as a sorrowful tale long past;
When Lord Lovell appeared the children cried,
"See! The old man weeps for his fairy bride."

At length, an oak chest that had long lain hid
Was found in the castle — they raised the lid
And a skeleton form lay mouldering there,
In the bridal wreath of that lady fair!
Oh, sad was her fate! In sportive jest
She hid from her lord in the old oak chest.
It closed with a spring! and, dreadful doom!
The bride lay clasped in her living tomb!

    I doubt if my mother would have recognized my version of this story.
There were times when I adapted my words to suit the multi-ethnicity of
the faces around me. On this occasion I shed the peaches-and-cream
English maiden with golden tresses — we'd had one of them the week
before, so it was time for Eastern dark eyes and long black silken locks. I
can't recall how I explained the fact that this Oxfordshire village beauty
who so entranced the young Lord Lovell was called Yasmin and had
originated in India, but that's how it was — much to the satisfaction of
several of the pupils of Asian origin in my story group. I had made her the
gentlest and bravest of heroines who many a time had cheated Death of a
trapped animal or a poor starved traveller.
    As love blossomed and the wedding day drew nigh, I paused in my
storytelling with these words:

    So happy was the beautiful Yasmin that she cried aloud, "I am afraid of
nothing and no one, not even of Death himself!"
    Death chuckled. "How little she knows my ways," he muttered. "I'll get her
on the very day she is wed." And he did.

    I suggested that the boys, in pairs or threes, work out what might
happen next. There was no need to warn them that she must not be run
over by a bus or burnt alive by a faulty electric blanket; Yasmin's ethos
stayed with them until we dispersed for our weekend. I am sorry now, in

retrospect, that I recorded only the facts of their ideas in my notebook, rather than their actual voices on tape. Here, at any rate, are those facts:

Hitesh: In the castle grounds a cat climbed to the top of the tallest tree and could not get down. Yasmin went up to rescue it and when she was up there Death created a great wind and she fell to her death.

Berkand: Yasmin heard the squealing of a rabbit in a snare. Death had disguised himself as the rabbit and as she reached down he rose up and stole her away.

Zahid: The wedding feast is in full swing and a young man appears with a fine wedding cake. He invites Yasmin to take and eat the first slice. She does and she dies. The man fades into a mist. The man is Death.

Jason: The wedding service takes place and at the very moment the ring is slipped onto her finger they turn towards each other. Yasmin sees into the eyes of Death and falls to the floor. Death is Lord Lovell.

Kevin: Yasmin drinks from the wedding goblet. She dies and looks into the wine and faintly sees in it the form of Death with his scythe.

Every one an acceptable ending. Each version delivered with a serious and fitting intensity. Such is the idiom of the story told. Such is its symbolism. Such are the things that drew the boys eagerly to my room at the weary end of the week. Truanting urges were stilled. Discipline came in the shape of expectation. Ex- or non-members of the group would sometimes turn up, little begging waifs and strays, so the circle of chairs would shuffle larger to accommodate them.

■ BABA YAGA

The awareness of the ethnic origins of my pupils was not something to be switched on and off or addressed only from time to time when I was thinking about course content in relation to "multi-cultural education"; it was part of the very texture of all our interactions, constantly enriching the daily experience of sharing our lives. It seemed to me that it would be both wasteful and discourteous to ignore our own identities; in any case, it would have been most unnatural to do so.

Many stories told on Friday afternoons had very precise ethnic locations: West Africa's Anansi stepped in, of course, on more than one occasion, and my own upbringing in Wales gave me the excuse to emphasize a Welsh accent for such stories as that of Gelert, the faithful dog buried at Beddgelert in north Wales. I would tell my pupils that, like the older members of their families, the stories had travelled from Greece or Italy or Nigeria or wherever. And there were some that came from everywhere: Abit, a non-English-speaking Turkish-Cypriot pupil in my first-year English class, would not be convinced that Ali, the boy who cried "Wolf!"

in a story we were working on, was not just a Turkish-Cypriot village boy like himself! In one story I told, when a princess was enormously helped in her search for the land where her wounded love lay bleeding by finding herself tucked in the secret branches of a dark cedar tree where a gaggle of witches habitually met to discuss what was going on in the world, I used the opportunity to extol the beauties of the countries of my pupils' origin (carefully researched beforehand) in the course of the witch sisters' boastful gossip.

At times I would change the wording of stories I read to adapt to our own situation. In Prince Ivan's story, which follows, Prince Ivan's father says to his luckless son, "See, you have a little sister; a fine girl she is too. She has teeth already. It's a pity they are black but time will put that right . . ." I just couldn't allow black to be a pity; in that group, a third of whom were West Indian in origin, black was beautiful and I would take no risks, not even with teeth! Generally, however, I was content to stay close to the exact wording of the stories which I read and chose to use.

One great source for stories was *Old Peter's Russian Tales*, collected and retold by Arthur Ransome. These tales have enormous appeal, especially those about Baba Yaga, the witch with iron teeth. They show how moved Ransome was by the poetic elements in Russian folklore, and how clearly he gobbled up every one of Baba Yaga's traditional features. Baba Yaga may be far distant from Tottenham, England, but she drew and clustered an intrigued audience around her.

"Tell us about Baba Yaga," begged Maroosia.

"Yes," said Vanya, "please, grandfather, and about the little hut on hen's legs."

"Baba Yaga is a witch," said old Peter, "a terrible old woman she is, but some-times kind enough. You know it was she who told Prince Ivan how to win one of the daughters of the Tsar of the Sea, and that was the best daughter of the bunch, Vasilissa the Very Wise. But then Baba Yaga is usually bad, as in the case of Vasilissa the Very Beautiful, who was only saved from her iron teeth by the cleverness of her Magic Doll."

"Tell us the story of the Magic Doll," begged Maroosia.

"I will some day," said old Peter.

"And has Baba Yaga really got iron teeth?" asked Vanya.

"Iron, like the poker and tongs," said old Peter.

"What for?" said Maroosia.

"To eat up little children," said old Peter, "when she can get them. She usu-ally only eats bad ones because the good ones get away. She is bony all over, and her eyes flash, and she drives about in a mortar, beating it with a pestle, and sweeping up her tracks with a besom, so that you cannot tell which way she has gone."

"And her hut?" said Vanya. He had often heard about it before, but he wanted to hear about it again.

"She lives in a little hut which stands on hen's legs. Sometimes it faces
the forest, sometimes it faces the path, and sometimes it walks solemnly about.
But in some of the stories she lives in another kind of hut, with a railing of
tall sticks, and a skull on each stick. And all night long fire glows in the skulls
and fades as the dawn rises."

And who could resist the language of this passage from the story
of Sadko, who, like Prince Ivan, is one of Old Peter's heroes?

"Play on," said the Tsar of the Sea, and he strode through the gates. The
sturgeons guarding the gates stirred the water with their tails.

And if the Tsar of the Sea was huge in his hall, he was huger still when
he stood outside on the bottom of the sea. He grew taller and taller, towering
like a mountain. His feet were like small hills. His blue hair hung down to
his waist, and he was covered with green scales. And he began to dance on the
bottom of the sea.

Great was that dancing. The sea boiled, and the ships went down. The
waves rolled as big as houses. The sea overflowed its shores and whole towns
were under water as the Tsar danced mightily on the bottom of the sea. Hither
and thither rushed the waves, and the very earth shook at the dancing of that
tremendous Tsar.

But the hugeness of that Tzar is nothing to the hugeness of the
involuntary suspension of disbelief which occurs in listeners to the story
told, rather than read. My pupils lived in the world of Sadko, not in the
world of the room in which we sat, and like all our stories, this one
produced a most delightful end to the working week.

■ PRINCE IVAN, THE WITCH BABY
AND THE LITTLE SISTER OF THE SUN

I want to quote this story in full because it is the one my younger secondary
pupils made most of in talk, writing and drama. It rivetted my little circle
of twelve- and thirteen-year-olds on a grey February afternoon in 1983.

Once upon a time, a very long time ago, there was a little Prince Ivan who was
dumb. Never a word had he spoken since the day that he was born — not so much
as a "Yes" or a "No," or a "Please" or a "Thank you." A great sorrow he was to his father
because he could not speak. Indeed, neither his father nor his mother could bear the
sight of him, for they thought, "A poor sort of Tzar will a dumb boy make!" They
even prayed, and said, "If only we could have another child, whatever it is like, it
could be no worse than this tongue-tied brat who cannot say a word." And for that
wish they were punished, as you shall hear. And they took no sort of care of the
little Prince Ivan, and he spent all his time in the stables, listening to the tales of
an old groom.

He was a wise man was the old groom, and he knew the past and the future, and what was happening under the earth. Maybe he had learnt his wisdom from the horses. Anyway, he knew more than other folk, and there came a day when he said to Prince Ivan:

"Little Prince," says he, "today you have a sister, and a bad one at that. She has come because of your father's prayers and your mother's wishes. A witch she is, and she will grow like a seed of corn. In six weeks she'll be a grown witch, and with her iron teeth she will eat up your father, and eat up your mother, and eat up you too, if she gets a chance. There's no saving the old people; but if you are quick, and do what I tell you, you may escape, and keep your soul in your body. And I love you, my little dumb Prince, and do not wish to think of your little body between her iron teeth. You must go to your father and ask him for the best horse he has, and then gallop like the wind, and away to the end of the world."

The little Prince ran off and found his father. There was his father, and there was his mother, and a little baby girl was in his mother's arms, screaming like a little fury.

"Well, she's not dumb," said his father, as if he were well pleased.

"Father," says the little Prince, "may I have the fastest horse in the stable?" And these were the first words that ever left his mouth.

"What!" says his father, "have you got a voice at last? Yes, take whatever horse you want. And see, you have a little sister; a fine girl she is too. She has teeth already. It's a pity they are black, but time will put that right, and it's better to have black teeth than to be born dumb."

Little Prince Ivan shook in his shoes when he heard of the black teeth of his little sister, for he knew that they were iron. He thanked his father and ran off to the stable. The old groom saddled the finest horse there was. Such a horse you never saw. Black it was, and its saddle and bridle were trimmed with shining silver. Little Prince Ivan climbed up and sat on the great black horse, and waved his hand to the old groom, and galloped away, on and on over the wide world.

"It's a big place, this world," thought the little Prince. "I wonder when I shall come to the end of it." You see, he had never been outside the palace grounds. And he had only ridden a little Finnish pony. And now he sat up, perched on the back of the great black horse, who galloped with hoofs that thundered beneath him, and leapt over rivers and streams and hillocks, and anything else that came in his way.

On and on galloped the little Prince on the great black horse. There were no houses anywhere to be seen. It was a long time since they had passed any people, and little Prince Ivan began to feel very lonely, and to wonder if indeed he had come to the end of the world, and could bring his journey to an end.

Suddenly, on a wide sandy plain, he saw two old, old women sitting in the road.

They were bent double over their work, sewing and sewing, and now one and now the other broke a needle, and took a new one out of the box between them and threaded the needle with thread from another box, and went on sewing and sewing. Their old noses nearly touched their knees as they bent over their work.

Little Prince Ivan pulled up the great black horse in a cloud of dust and spoke to the old women.

"Grandmothers," said he, "is this the end of the world? Let me stay here and live with you, and be safe from my baby sister, who is a witch and has iron teeth. Please let me stay with you, and I'll be very little trouble, and thread your needles for you when you break them."

"Prince Ivan, my dear," said one of the old women, "this is not the end of the world, and little good would it be to you to stay with us. For as soon as we have broken all our needles and used up all our thread, we shall die, and then where would you be? Your sister with the iron teeth would have you in a minute."

The little Prince cried bitterly, for he was very little and all alone. He rode on farther over the wide world, the black horse galloping and galloping, and throwing dust from his thundering hoofs.

He came into a forest of great oaks, the biggest oak trees in the whole world. And in that forest was a dreadful noise — the crashing of trees falling, the breaking of branches, and the whistling of things hurled through the air. The Prince rode on, and there before him was the huge giant, Tree-rooter, hauling the great oaks out of the ground and flinging them aside like weeds.

"I should be safe with him," thought little Prince Ivan, "and this, surely, must be the end of the world."

He rode close up under the giant, stopped the black horse, and shouted up into the air.

"Please, great giant," says he, "is this the end of the world? And may I live with you and be safe from my sister, who is a witch, and grows like a seed of corn, and has iron teeth?"

"Prince Ivan, my dear," says Tree-rooter, "this is not the end of the world, and little good would it be to you to stay with me, for as soon as I have rooted up all these trees I shall die, and then where would you be? Your sister would have you in a minute. And already there are not many big trees left."

And the giant set to work again, pulling up the great trees and throwing them aside. The sky was full of flying trees.

Little Prince Ivan cried bitterly, for he was very little and he was all alone. He rode on farther over the wide world, the black horse galloping and galloping under the tall trees, and throwing clods of earth from his thundering hoofs.

He came among the mountains. And there was a roaring and a crashing in the mountains as if the earth was falling to pieces. One after another whole mountains were lifted up into the sky and flung down to earth, so that they broke and scattered into dust. And the big black horse galloped through the mountains, and the little Prince sat bravely on his back. And there, close before him, was the huge giant, Mountain-tosser, picking up the mountains like pebbles and hurling them to little pieces and dust upon the ground.

"This must be the end of the world," thought the little Prince; "and at any rate I should be safe with him."

"Please, great giant," says he, "is this the end of the world? And may I live with you and be safe from my sister, who is a witch, and has iron teeth, and grows like a seed of corn?"

"Prince Ivan, my dear," says Mountain-tosser, resting for a moment and dusting the rocks from his great hands, "this is not the end of the world, and little good would it be to you to stay with me. For as soon as I have picked up all these mountains and thrown them down again I shall die, and then where would you be?

Your sister would have you in a minute. And there are not very many mountains left."

And the giant set to work again, lifting up the great mountains and hurling them away. The sky was full of flying mountains.

Little Prince Ivan wept bitterly, for he was very little and was all alone. He rode on farther over the wide world, the black horse galloping and galloping over the mountain paths, and throwing stones from his thundering hoofs.

At last he came to the end of the world, and there, hanging in the sky above him, was the castle of the little sister of the Sun. Beautiful it was, made of cloud, and hanging in the sky as if it were built of red roses.

"I should be safe up there," thought little Prince Ivan, and just then the Sun's little sister opened the window and beckoned to him.

Prince Ivan patted the big black horse and whispered to it, and it leapt up high into the air and through the window, into the very courtyard of the castle.

"Stay here and play with me," said the little sister of the Sun; and Prince Ivan tumbled off the big black horse into her arms, and laughed because he was so happy.

Merry and pretty was the Sun's little sister, and she was very kind to Prince Ivan. They played games together, and when she was tired she let him do whatever he liked and run about her castle. This way and that he ran about the battlements of rosy cloud, hanging in the sky over the end of the world.

But one day he climbed up and up to the topmost turret of the castle. From there he could see the whole world. And far away, beyond the mountains, beyond the forests, beyond the wide plains, he saw his father's palace where he had been born. The roof of the palace was gone, and the walls were broken and crumbling. And little Prince Ivan came slowly down from the turret, and his eyes were red with weeping.

"My dear," says the Sun's little sister, "why are your eyes so red?"

"It is the wind up there," says liitle Prince Ivan.

And the Sun's little sister put her head out of the window of the castle of cloud and whispered to the winds not to blow so hard.

But next day little Prince Ivan went up again to the topmost turret, and looked far away over the wide world to the ruined palace. "She has eaten them all with her iron teeth," he said to himself. And his eyes were red when he came down.

"My dear," says the Sun's little sister, "your eyes are red again."

"It is the wind," says little Prince Ivan.

And the Sun's little sister put her head out of the window and scolded the wind.

But the third day again little Prince Ivan climbed up the stairs of cloud to that topmost turret, and looked far away to the broken palace where his father and mother had lived. And he came down from the turret with tears running down his face.

"Why, you are crying, my dear!" says the Sun's little sister. "Tell me what it is all about."

So little Prince Ivan told the little sister of the Sun how his sister was a witch, and how he wept to think of his father and mother, and how he had seen the ruins of his father's palace far away, and how he could not stay with her happily until he knew how it was with his parents.

"Perhaps it is not too late to save them from her iron teeth, though the old groom said that she would certainly eat them, and that it was the will of God. But let me ride back on my big black horse."

"Do not leave me, my dear," says the Sun's little sister. "I am lonely here by myself."

"I will ride back on my big black horse, and then I will come to you again."

"What must be, must," says the Sun's little sister, "though she is more likely to eat you than you are to save them. You shall go. But you must take with you a magic comb, a magic brush, and two apples of youth. These apples would make young once more the oldest things on earth."

Then she kissed little Prince Ivan, and he climbed on his big black horse, and leapt out of the window of the castle down on the end of the world, and galloped off on his way back over the wide world.

He came to Mountain-tosser, the giant. There was only one mountain left, and the giant was just picking it up. Sadly he was picking it up, for he knew that when he had thrown it away his work would be done and he would have to die.

"Well, little Prince Ivan," says Mountain-tosser, "this is the end;" and he heaves up the mountain. But before he could toss it away the little Prince threw his magic brush on the plain, and the brush swelled and burst, and there were range upon range of high mountains, touching the sky itself.

"Why," says Mountain-tosser, "I have enough mountains now to last me for another thousand years. Thank you kindly, little Prince."

And he set to work again, heaving up mountains and tossing them down, while little Prince Ivan galloped on across the wide world.

He came to Tree-rooter, the giant. There were only two of the great oaks left, and the giant had one in each hand.

"Ah me, little Prince Ivan," says Tree-rooter, "my life is come to its end; for I have only to pluck up these two trees and throw them down, and then I shall die."

"Pluck them up," says little Prince Ivan. "Here are plenty more for you." And he threw down his comb. There was a noise of spreading branches, of swishing leaves, of opening buds, all together, and there before them was a forest of great oaks stretching farther than the giant could see, tall though he was.

"Why," says Tree-rooter, "here are enough trees to last me for another thousand years. Thank you kindly, little Prince."

And he set to work again, pulling up the big trees, laughing joyfully and hurling them over his head, while little Prince Ivan galloped on across the wide world.

He came to the two old women. They were crying their eyes out.

"There is only one needle left!" says the first.

"There is only one bit of thread in the box!" sobs the second.

"And then we shall die!" they say both together, mumbling with their old mouths.

"Before you use the needle and thread, just eat these apples," says little Prince Ivan, and he gives them the two apples of youth.

The two old women took the apples in their shaking fingers and ate them, bent double, mumbling with their old lips. They had hardly finished their last mouthfuls when they sat up straight, smiled with sweet red lips, and looked at the little Prince with shining eyes. They had become young girls again, and their grey hair was black as the raven.

"Thank you kindly, little Prince," say the two young girls. "You must take with you the handkerchief we have been sewing all these years. Throw it to the ground, and it will turn into a lake of water. Perhaps some day it will be useful to you."

"Thank you," says the little Prince, and off he gallops, on and on over the wide world.

He came at last to his father's palace. The roof was gone, and there were holes in the walls. He left his horse at the edge of the garden, and crept up to the ruined palace and peeped through a hole. Inside, in the great hall, was sitting a huge baby girl, filling the whole hall. There was no room for her to move. She had knocked off the roof with a shake of her head. And she sat there in the ruined hall, sucking her thumb.

And while Prince Ivan was watching through the hole, he heard her mutter to herself:

"Eaten the father, eaten the mother,
And now to eat the little brother."

And she began shrinking, getting smaller and smaller every minute.

Little Prince Ivan had only just time to get away from the hole in the wall when a pretty little baby girl came running out of the ruined palace.

"You must be my little brother Ivan," she called out to him, and came up to him smiling. But as she smiled the little Prince saw that her teeth were black; and as she shut her mouth he heard them clink together like pokers.

"Come in," says she, and she took little Prince Ivan with her to a room in the palace, all broken down and cobwebbed. There was a dulcimer lying in the dust on the floor.

"Well, little brother," says the witch baby, "you play on the dulcimer and amuse yourself while I get supper ready. But don't stop playing, or I shall feel lonely." And she ran off, and left him.

Little Prince Ivan sat down and played tunes on the dulcimer — sad enough tunes. You would not play dance music if you thought you were going to be eaten by a witch.

But while he was playing a little grey mouse came out of a crack in the floor. Some people think that this was the wise old groom, who had turned into a little grey mouse to save Ivan from the witch baby.

"Ivan, Ivan," says the little grey mouse, "run while you may. Your father and mother were eaten long ago, and well they deserved it. But be quick, or you will be eaten too. Your pretty little sister is putting an edge on her teeth!"

Little Prince Ivan thanked the mouse, and ran out from the ruined palace, and climbed up on the back of his big black horse, with its saddle and bridle trimmed with silver. Away he galloped over the wide world. The witch baby stopped her work and listened. She heard the music of the dulcimer, so she made sure he was still there. She went on sharpening her teeth with a file, and growing bigger and bigger every minute. And all the time the music of the dulcimer sounded among the ruins.

As soon as her teeth were quite sharp she rushed off to eat little Prince Ivan. She tore aside the walls of the room. There was nobody there — only a little grey mouse running and jumping this way and that on the strings of the dulcimer.

When it saw the witch baby the little mouse ran across the floor and into the crack and away, so that she never caught it. How the witch baby gnashed her teeth! Poker and tongs, poker and tongs — what a noise they made! She swelled up, bigger and bigger, till she was a baby as high as the palace. And then she jumped up so that the palace fell to pieces about her. Then off she ran after little Prince Ivan.

Little Prince Ivan, on the big black horse, heard a noise behind him. He looked back, and there was the huge witch, towering over the trees. She was dressed like a little baby, and her eyes flashed and her teeth clanged as she shut her mouth. She was running with long strides, faster than the black horse could gallop — and he was the best horse in all the world.

Little Prince Ivan threw down the handkerchief that had been sewn by the two old women who had eaten the apples of youth. It turned into a deep, broad lake, so that the witch baby had to swim — and swimming is slower than running. It took her a long time to get across, and all that time Prince Ivan was galloping on, never stopping for a moment.

The witch baby crossed the lake and came thundering after him. Close behind she was, and would have caught him; but the giant Tree-rooter saw the little Prince galloping on the big black horse, and the witch baby tearing after him. He pulled up the great oaks in armfuls, and threw them down just in front of the witch baby. He made a huge pile of big trees, and the witch baby had to stop and gnaw her way through them with her big iron teeth.

It took her a long time to gnaw through the trees, and the black horse galloped and galloped ahead. But presently Prince Ivan heard a noise behind him. He looked back, and there was the witch baby, thirty feet high, racing after him, clanging with her teeth. Close behind she was, and the little Prince sat firm on the big black horse, and galloped and galloped. But she would have caught him if the giant Mountain-tosser had not seen the little Prince on the big black horse, and the great witch baby running after him. The giant tore up the biggest mountain in the world and flung it down in front of her, and another on the top of that. She had to bite her way through them, while the little Prince galloped and galloped.

At last little Prince Ivan saw the cloud castle of the little sister of the Sun, hanging over the end of the world and gleaming in the sky as if it were made of roses. He shouted with hope, and the black horse shook his head proudly and galloped on. The witch baby thundered after him. Nearer she came and nearer.

"Ah, little one," screams the witch baby, "you shan't get away this time!"

The Sun's little sister was looking from a window of the castle in the sky, and she saw the witch baby stretching out to grab little Prince Ivan. She flung the window open, and just in time the big black horse leapt up, and through the window and into the courtyard, with little Prince Ivan safe on its back.

How the witch baby gnashed her iron teeth!

"Give him up!" she screams.

"I will not!" says the Sun's little sister.

"See you here," says the witch baby, and she makes herself smaller and smaller and smaller, till she was just like a real little girl. "Let us be weighed in the great scales, and if I am heavier than Prince Ivan, I can take him; and if he is heavier than I am, I'll say no more about it."

The Sun's little sister laughed at the witch baby and teased her, and she hung the great scales out of the cloud castle so that they swung above the end of the world.

Little Prince Ivan got into one scale, and down it went.

"Now," said the witch baby, "we shall see."

And she made herself bigger and bigger and bigger, till she was as big as she had been when she sat and sucked her thumb in the hall of the ruined palace. "I am the heavier," she shouted, and gnashed her iron teeth. Then she jumped into the other scale.

She was so heavy that the scale with the little Prince in it shot up into the air. It shot up so fast that little Prince Ivan flew up into the sky, up and up and up, and came down on the topmost turret of the cloud castle of the little sister of the Sun.

The Sun's little sister laughed, and closed the window, and went up to the turret to meet the little Prince. But the witch baby turned back the way she had come, and went off, gnashing her iron teeth until they broke.

And ever since then little Prince Ivan and the little sister of the Sun play together in the castle of cloud that hangs over the end of the world. They borrow the stars to play at ball, and put them back at night whenever they remember.

"So when there are no stars?" asked Maroosia?

"It means that Prince Ivan and the Sun's little sister have gone to sleep over their games and forgotten to put their toys away."

It seems too long since I told this story, for it is a gem of a tale, fit for any age. All it demands is a suspension of sophistication: accept the sense of inevitability provided by Prince Ivan's repeated pleas as he moves tearfully towards the end of the world the first time; be moved by his lonely isolation; be joyful at the wonder of the place and the playtime he reaches. Note the succession of striking images — the small child tightly clasped to his black mount beneath the towering figure of a giant; clouds that make a pink vision of a castle in the air; a grotesque mass of flesh in the shape of a baby girl, filling her stone frame; an expanse of forest, a mountain range, a shimmering lake, which emerge from nowhere. And magic all the way, echoing magic from stories in our own long ago, some familiar, some only intimated on the edge of memory. When all's done, evil is not destroyed; conservationists or no, forests will disappear; a thousand years will pass and every mountain and hill will be laid low; old age advances ever and the thread of life runs out; Death will arrive at last, as it did several stories later in my weekly storytelling. In the meantime of this story, however, there is beauty, enterprise, hope, loyalty, gratitude, caritas and glorious fantasy.

■ VISITING STORYTELLERS

A bonus for all of us was each occasion when I invited an outsider to tell a story. Yasmin was placed deliberately the week before my friend John Richmond was due to come to tell his version of *The Pardoner's Tale*. I hoped that via storyteller Minster Lovell my pupils would be ready for the attempt of the three drunken youths to track down Death in the shape of the Plague. My husband revealed some secrets in a true story of an occasion when, in detention at school, his suave man-of-the-world classmate Hoffman let off the fire extinguisher. Then there was my colleague and friend Renrick Henry from St. Vincent, who was to oblige my classes on many an occasion with an Anansi story, or one from his own life. When Tony Lenney, the Chief Education Officer of the locality, mentioned during a visit to the school that he regretted not getting into the classroom much, it didn't take long to persuade him to be a Friday afternoon visiting storyteller. He told us of sparrows from the north of England, alias dunnocks; of a cotton mill filled with so much din it turned his auntie into a deaf but fully trained lip-reader; and of a blizzard which forced him to spend an unexpected night on a bare mountain.

I also wrote letters home to the parents of each new batch of second years with an invitation to become a storyteller for our group, but, alas, no one ever responded. Perhaps those letters fell out of plastic bags or disappeared down grids; or perhaps secondary schools are not considered very attractive places to venture into.

Little did I know when I began storytelling that, by hook or by crook, it would make that particular school more attractive for me in times to come, or that my resolve would stick with me even when staffing necessities drove me exclusively into preparing pupils for external examinations.

Three

CLASSROOM STORYTELLING

The expectations for English classes are enormous. Government reports are everywhere, not to speak of the millions of words written by theoreticians of various sorts, by academics, by researchers and, less often, by practicing teachers. It all adds up to a lot of painful demands on the pupils.

I had spent a lot of teaching years up to that point trying to eliminate pain and switch my pupils on. And that was precisely what I was up to in taking storytelling into the classroom. There was no doubt about what was required of the Friday afternoon story group: it was the place where stories were told, that's all. The only demands made on the pupils were that they sit, listen and tell. Before the story group was invented my Friday afternoons had not been remarkable for an excess of peace or productivity. If telling stories was the answer when the coming weekend set the pugging tooth on edge, how much more easily would it sit elsewhere in the working week?

The stories of this chapter come out of 1/U, a "regular" English classroom. One factor that provided the right soil for storytelling in that group was the supportive, collaborative atmosphere among the pupils. Nothing could better illustrate this than the story of Abit, a young Turkish boy whose sudden arrival in 1/U raised all sorts of challenges.

Abit spoke Greek and Turkish, his mother tongue and another in which he was quite literate, but he knew no English at all. He was withdrawn from most lessons to get individual help from Pete Whetman, the ESL specialist, but it seemed right that he should be in the mainstream as much as possible and that English lessons should be one area to include him. The first thing I asked him to do was write a story he knew, in Turkish. I knew this device would work because I had already encountered a non-English-speaking Turkish boy — Mehmet — in a different class, and when he was asked through a pupil interpreter to do just that for me, the expression on his face was totally transformed from numb apathy to a smile of real pleasure. I can still see that moment in my head if I think about it. It is so easy — and so dangerous — to treat such pupils as though they are illiterate simply because they can't write English.

Abit was lucky in two respects. He had two props: Pete Whetman, who would come into the classroom with him, and Erkan, an extraordinarily sociable Turkish-speaking lad, fluently bilingual, who instantly took Abit under his wing. If Abit was ever bullied or mocked (this never happened in 1/U but occasionally did in the melee of the school playground), Erkan would be the leader of an angry posse of classmates, a protective arm round Abit's shoulders, to seek me out — but not unless his own illicit punch-up in Abit's defence had proved unsuccessful.

Abit arrived in December and it wasn't until well on into the Easter term that I launched into a storytelling phase in that classroom. By then he had got used to being included in other ways, occasionally even being the star. Once I decided to use a dual-text worksheet from the second-language learner workpack *The World in a City* so the whole class could see what Turkish looked like in print. Abit often read to me in Turkish, and Erkan (who was not nearly so hot in this respect) was enormously proud of his protégé's skill. Many a visitor to the classroom was startled to find himself dragged by the arm Abit-wards and instructed to sit and listen to Abit reading aloud in what was as much double-dutch to the visitor as it was to me: a dubious treat, yet visitors always made appropriate congratulatory noises when he'd finished, encouraged no doubt by Erkan's gurgles of delight and Abit's shy smile. In class, Abit read aloud to everyone from the worksheet, which was about immigrant grandparents, followed by the same passages read in English by others. By the end of the lesson Abit was the centre of a busy group wanting to know which were the Turkish words for *family, daughter, friends, lonely*.

Hearing Abit read aloud must have given his classmates a sense of the patience of this quiet newcomer who sat silent through hours of alien gabble delivered by teachers and everyone else around him throughout the day. It also demonstrated that he was just as capably literate as they. Even on the topic of grandparents, selected by me simply because of the convenient worksheet, he had to suffer my serialized reading of "Granny Reardun" from *The Stone Book* by Alan Garner. It had caught these pupils up into its archaic rural setting even though it was quite foreign to them in time, place, dialect and pace. But it meant nothing to Abit, and Erkan was listening much too hard to transmit any meaning to his mate.

While I smiled, gestured and goggle-eyed my way through "Prince Ivan, the Witch Baby and the Little Sister of the Sun," Pete sweated over his note-taking. Then during the last twenty minutes of the lesson Pete, Erkan and Abit went off in a little huddle to piece it all together. As I expected, the story went down quite well and occupied some very successful drama lessons with Abit making a very creditable Giant Tree-rooter.

In later stories I tried to assist Pete and Erkan by drawing pictures for Abit in advance of the storytelling. The first was an Italian story about yet another princess confined to a tower, except that in this case it was she who rescued the prince from certain death instead of the usual other way round, with the help of information gleaned from overhearing one of those witches I mentioned earlier who met under the cedar tree. I had drawn twenty or so pictures to help Abit with the story and was therefore somewhat chastened when Erkan told me later that he'd got lost somewhere round the third one. But the time was certainly ripe to put Abit onto centre stage again.

■ ABIT'S STORY

Back to the story Abit wrote on his first day, which was a short, conventional version of the familiar story about the boy who always lied. Together the whole class heard the translation of Abit's story:

> Once upon a time there was a boy called Ali. Every day Ali looked after the sheep from morning till night. One day when he was looking after the sheep he thought of an idea to shout "Wolf!" and make all the farmers and farmers' wives come running towards him to see what was going on. He shouted, "Wolf! Wolf!" and some of the farmers came with big sticks and what did they see? There wasn't a wolf to be seen. And the people that Ali had tricked shouted out, "Liar! Liar!"
>
> A few weeks later everyone had forgotten about what had happened. Again he was looking after the sheep and he wanted to trick the farmers again. "Wolf! Wolf!" he cried, and the farmers that heard him all got their sticks and ran towards him, but there was no wolf in sight. They all started shouting "Liar! Liar!" again. "You'll never be able to trick us again," they said, "because we won't believe you next time." From then on they called him "the Liar."
>
> One day when Ali was looking after the sheep, a pack of wolves started to attack the sheep. Ali the Liar screamed, "Wolf! Wolf! Wolf!" but the people that heard him took no notice and didn't go running towards him. And the wolf ripped Ali apart and started to eat him.

A good deal of time was spent discussing how this sequence of events might have affected different members of the village community. I asked the boys to write their own versions of these events from the point of view of one of the villagers. To help them, I told them the beginning as I might do it:

Our village is a quiet place. Nothing very unusual happens. Births, deaths, marriages, gossip, arguments over how the crops will fare or how the lambing's coming along. There's plenty to do; even the young children take their share of the jobs. There was one young 'un who came to a bad end, though.

It all started one day when I was clearing a ditch down by the old mill. It was too full of weed and rubbish to flow along right. Chilly day it was — the wind was howling round my ears and my fingers were numb. I straightened my back just for a moment — and there was old Jim and his little lad Ali, both making for the big meadow where Jim kept his flock of sheep. Reckon Jim was going to give him a lesson in shepherding.

Later that day . . .

The only other instruction was that they were to make sure they knew exactly who they were and the kind of day it was when the events took place.

I have no doubt at all that had I lectured them on the theoretical structure of the story, rather than giving them a little sample bit after the discussion, the results from 1/U would have been very different. Dennis, for one, whose story is reproduced in full below, would have written nothing; he might even have scampered off. As it was, their stories were remarkable. Every child in that mixed-ability group produced something of real interest, and some stories were quite outstanding. The other boys were encouraged to believe that their success was due to Abit, the "source" of the material. But I knew it was the result of magic, the magic of narration itself — the telling, the retelling, the talking about, the dramatization of, the reflection upon — a gestalt of story.

■ DENNIS' STORY

Ali was a boy aged about ten. He was a bad boy who never stopped telling lies. He had the job of looking after the sheep. One day Ali's mum was going to the village.

"May I come too?" said Ali.

"No," said his mother. "You have been a bad boy lately and as a result you will not go to the village for a week." And with that she stomped out of the house.

Ali went up the hill to the sheep. Ali's dad was with the sheep, stick in one hand, gun in the other.

"May I look after the sheep now?" asked Ali.

"You may look after the sheep," I said.

"Thank you, father," said Ali to me.

As I walked down the hill I thought to myself, Ali will have to stop lying because one day something very bad will happen to him.

It was four o'clock in the evening. Ali sat there watching the sun set. As Ali did this he became bored.

"I'm bored," said Ali to himself. "I wish I could do something to liven things up a bit." Well, as Ali thought about this he had an idea. He would go to the top of the hill and shout "Wolf! Wolf!" That should liven things up a bit. And so Ali put his ideas into action and he ran to the very top of the hill and shouted, "There's a wolf! There's a wolf!"

Some farmers came out carrying guns and sticks. "Where is the wolf? Where is it?" But as we know, there was no wolf in sight for miles around. All there was were the trees whistling in the wind and the bright red sunset and of course there was Ali laughing his head off.

"Ali, you are a liar and one day a pack of wolves will come but we won't believe you for all liars must come to a bad end."

"No, no!" shouted Ali. "Nothing can happen to me and nothing never will!" he said in his stubborn way. But, alas, Ali was wrong as you will see later in the story.

The people said nothing but went back to their huts. The next morning all the farmers that had fallen for Ali's trick the night before came to complain to me about Ali.

"You are Ali's father, aren't you? Can't you keep the boy under control?" said a farmer to me. "One day something is going to happen to Ali when he is least expecting it."

"Well, I've thought about that," I said, "and if anything does happen to him it will be his own fault. There is only one thing for it. Leave him to learn the hard way."

All the farmers turned away and went home. Secretly I was very angry with Ali so I went up to the foot of the hill where I kept the sheep.

"Ali!" I shouted up, "I want to see you about something." I shouted but there was no answer. I walked up the hill and when I got to the top of it Ali was sitting under the shade of a tree near to where the sheep were. Ali seemed to be sleeping. I was just going to leave and see if the sheep were all right when Ali sneezed.

"I thought you were meant to be asleep! You were pretending, weren't you? Well you can't fool me. I want a word with you."

But Ali ran off down the hill, leaving me behind. "That boy!" I said to myself. "That boy!"

As the sun started to set Ali ran to the hill and started to hunt for his dad. Good. He wasn't there. Ali kept watch on the sheep. Ali then heard a howling sort of noise. It was nearby but Ali took no notice of it. And then something caught his eye. It was a brown slinky figure. Ali had seen that figure somewhere before. Now what was it? Then he remembered that howling noise he had heard and all at once a wolf jumped out of one of the bushes nearby and started to attack the sheep. He shouted, "Wolf! Wolf!" But of course nobody heard him. They didn't want to hear because they considered him a liar.

But somebody did hear his shouts and cries. Somebody ran up the hill with a gun in his hand, somebody who didn't know Ali was a liar, somebody who didn't ignore his shouts and cries. Somebody shot at the wolf who turned and ran away. It was a traveller, you see. The traveller had not been there the night before when Ali had told the lie about the wolf. So instead of ignoring the shouts and cries he reacted quickly.

"Thank you!" cried Ali. "You — you saved my life. But who are you and why did you come to my aid?"

"I came to your aid because I heard you shouting 'Wolf! Wolf!' You see I am a traveller and I stopped here to camp the night."

"Oh," said Ali, "that explains a lot."

"I think you had better go to the hospital for that cut. It seems to be bleeding badly. Did the wolf do it?"

"Yes," said Ali.

"Come on. I'll get a farmer to look after the sheep, then I'll go and tell your parents what happened and after that we can take you to the hospital. That's a deep cut, son."

And the traveller informed us what had happened. Next day his mum and I went to see Ali in hospital.

"I hope that taught you a lesson, son," I said.

"It did, dad, it did," he said.

"So it should," said Ali's mum.

"When you said nothing bad will happen to you you spoke too soon. Now, son, I don't know how to say this but I'll put it like this. All the farmers that you tricked when you shouted 'Wolf' would you please apologise to them and would you thank the traveller who saved you? And now, son, will you faithfully promise me that you'll never lie again — or at least *try* to stop lying?"

"I will, father. Last night was a night I shall never forget — well, at least not for a long, long, long, long time."

Stories sat easily enough upon Dennis Humphrey of 1/U. If anyone avoided the everyday it was Dennis. Life had to have oomph in it or he didn't give it a moment's pause. There was plenty about school that Dennis did not find altogether magnetizing, so playing truant or (to use the local patois) "bunking off" figured largely in his secondary days and was, so I was told, small fry compared with earlier goings on. During his third year, when I happened not to be involved with the class, I discovered by chance that bunking off school totally absorbed Dennis although the details, like Dennis, have escaped me. Unpredictable and volatile though he was in 1/U, he committed none of the atrocities augured by his primary school headteacher, including the threat that "he won't last three weeks in *that* school!"

I really liked Dennis. He had enormous talent as a teller of tales, both real and imaginary; he was a great source of fantasy, fun and laughter. He also had a fund of information on the doppies and rice-scatterings of Jamaican occult. In drama lessons his confidence was as massive as his voice was stentorian. He didn't mind singing some songs he knew either, though some of them had an uncomfortable ring of infiltrated Uncle Tom about them. But I didn't intrude.

Singing was one of the many acquisitions he inherited, I reckon, from his mum. She was a big lady with a soft and sweet high-pitched singing voice which she used for me and another first-year class once when we were having a drama lesson in the hall. She'd stumbled in on us while searching, yet again, for Dennis' latest hiding place: apparently he hadn't come home the night before. She sang a West Indian yard rhyme about a little brown girl sitting in a ring; there were lots of trilling tra la la's and a chorus line that went: "For she like sugar and I like plum." Then she and I talked about Dennis for a bit. I don't remember much of what she said, but there was a lot of it, interspersed with many a "That boy! That boy!" and "If I keep him in for a week it do no good" and "He say he sorry and he promise faithfully never to do it again but . . ." and "I just can't keep that boy under control. If anything happens to that boy it will be his own fault!" And so on.

Dennis was, like his friendly mother, decidedly oral. But writing — ah, there's the rub! Picking up a pen is a solitary business and was not among the attractions of school for the irrepressible Dennis. When he was really drawn into the task set, he would produce many pages of swift scrawl, keeping his head down until his chef d'oeuvre was complete. Complete, that is, but for a very occasional spelling correction which he had no objection to my incorporating, and *all* the punctuation, which he considered totally superfluous since he was perfectly capable of reading out everything he had written to his classmates with brilliantly appropriate intonation and colour. Then that was that. It was of no further interest to him. On no account would he revise, correct or "write it out in best," as we used to say at Clydach Junior School. These days, when drafting and redrafting is all the sanctified vogue, what price "success" for the likes of Dennis? And it isn't as if he stands alone: many an artist in paint or words is only interested in the task for as long as it is being created from scratch. Once the last drop of paint is plopped or word scribed, then it's on with the motley for the next performance.

His story was no mean achievement. For a first-year pupil it is a substantial piece of writing. For a "school refuser" it shows total commitment. For a boy largely rejected by the system it reveals a remarkable variety of acquired skills. Most obviously, Dennis is fluent and economical throughout:

Ali's dad was with the sheep, stick in one hand, gun in the other.

All there was were the trees whistling in the wind and the bright red sunset and of course there was Ali laughing his head off.

But of course nobody heard him. They didn't want to hear because they considered him a liar.

He is able to draw his reader in and onwards:

. . . Ali will have to stop lying because one day something very bad will happen to him.

But as we know, there was no wolf in sight for miles around.

But, alas, Ali was wrong as you will see later in the story.

. . . one day a pack of wolves will come . . .

. . . leave him to learn the hard way . . .

He shows a strong sense of drama:

As the sun started to set Ali ran to the hill and started to hunt for his dad. Good. He wasn't there.

And then something caught his eye. It was a brown slinky figure. Ali had seen that figure somewhere before. Now what was it? Then he remembered that howling noise he had heard . . .

The most spectacular example is the episode of Ali's rescue with the "somebody" repeated and finally explained, which I think is quite masterly.

Another "literary" device he uses, apparently instinctively, is switching between the voice of the narrator and the voice of the father.

Dennis read only sporadically. I am quite convinced that all these skills were the result partly of his perceptive intelligence and partly of his contact with an oral culture, reinforced and confirmed by hearing stories told in class.

■ OTHER STORIES

The other pupils produced some outstanding work as well. Nicholas began like this:

The sun rose over the hill and the flowers seemed to come alive.

Nobody had instructed him in the craft of story openings.

Here are some extracts from Chris's story:

It was a cold, chilly day. I was mending shoes in the shop. I worked as a cobbler, fixing shoes, putting new soles on, fixing heels. Normally it's not a busy day but today it was very busy, people coming in and out, until, about 3.00 pm, I heard "Wolf! Wolf!" . . .

. . . I tried to get to the front. I heard Ali's voice. He said, "I've tricked you! You all came thinking there was a wolf but there isn't really." The villagers all came back, mumbling to themselves.

It did not take a formal grammar lesson on the use of participial phrases for Chris to be able to use one effectively.

Che, like one or two others, responded to my reminder of village life in Garner's "Granny Reardun." Here are three extracts from what was probably the most impressive retelling of Abit's tale:

"Everybody get your sticks and guns. I'll get my forge hammer and batter or destroy the vermins!"

Soon after I was back at work. The clang of metal against metal is like music to my ears — steam, smoke, sweat, the bellows are puffing! Four more horseshoes today and then I'm finished.

" 'Tis I, Ali!"

"Everybody get him! Let him be beaten with a hand as rough as coal yet as hard as steel!"

Che did not have a lesson on similes: could it be that simply hearing them used in the cheerful context of storytelling time was enough to get the message across? Should I not have been concerning myself about his reading age? Would his words have proved as meaningful had they been the responses to a standardized test?

But I get carried away — as I may well have done in my estimation of 1/U as a whole. Colleagues would tell me I exaggerated their strengths just because they were my tutor group. However, I was never again to have a class that I cared for as much. Somehow everything I planned seemed to work with them: that was why I could not be absolutely sure that there was anything special, educationally, about storytelling. Learning, whether it was conventional school stuff or all about people and living, became a shared, mutually supportive matter. From the start they shared their original writings, reading them aloud to each other in clusters or in one big group at the front, the tables abandoned at the back of the room. One individual's problem became a problem for the whole group, whether it was a mislaid digital watch, difficulty over putting periods in the right places, fear of being "taxed" (this was a form of extortion by bullying), injustice encountered anywhere, X's moments of violent tantrum, Y's fits of hysteria, Z's sickle-cell anaemia, sickness, disagreements of any sort. Things were talked through and many a solution was mutually discovered. I was never aware of any competitiveness while I was with them, although it would be silly to claim it did not exist.

It was here that Abit read out his very first piece of extended writing in English. I forget the details of the content but remember distinctly that 2/C (as they were called by then) listened, still as stones, until he stopped and glanced doubtfully up at me for approval. That was when, to a man, they spontaneously clapped for him. Six months later Abit's guardian shifted him to a different school; he could not take Erkan with him, of course, or the solidarity of that small community of classmates, and for that reason alone I cannot imagine that it was a wise move.

I saw the group only for morning and afternoon registration each day (twenty-five minutes or so) and three double lessons (three and a half hours) of English each week. They were young enough to take their cue from me during those times, and it was my genuine belief that each person had his individual qualities to contribute to the whole. Grading of any kind, with either letters or marks out of ten, was simply not on the agenda in any of my lessons. Words to praise what was of value — and, of course, at times to point out weaknesses to be remedied — were much more productive than creating an atmosphere where "What mark did you get?" would replace "Let me read what you wrote" at the moment their exercise books were returned to them.

My deepest regret is that when I had a chance to get Dennis Humphrey back again, as a 4, he had disappeared for good.

Four

MAKING USE OF UNLIKELY STORIES

■ MICHAEL'S STORY

Once there was a king who promised he would never chop anyone's head off. He ruled over a very noisy court. Everyone made a noise. They laughed and shouted and sang. They coughed. They hiccupped. They banged and thumped. They booed. They whistled and cheered.

Now the king didn't like the noise and he wanted to stop it. So he thought a bit and he walked a bit. He thought a bit more — and then he had a plan.

"The next one of you to make a noise will die!" he said.

Everyone went quiet, even though they all knew this king would never chop anyone's head off.

Everyone went quiet — except in one corner, and there was the boy who scrubbed the pots and pans in the kitchen. He was new to the court, and he made a noise and laughed. He liked noise.

The king looked at him. Everyone looked at him. He laughed again.

"Boy! Leave the hall!" the king said.

So the boy picked himself up and went off to the kitchens.

"Guards! Lock the doors!"

The guards locked the doors. The king sat and waited. The court sat and waited. Outside, the boy banged his saucepan and sang.

> Up and down
> Up and down
> Tim Tom Tackler
> Goes up and down.

A whole hour went by. Not a sound came from inside the hall. Dinner time came, and still everyone was quiet. But outside they could hear the boy's song.

> Up and down
> Up and down
> Tim Tom Tackler
> Goes up and down.

Everyone was quiet, and now they could hear the boy eating. They could hear the sound of a ladle hitting the big soup cauldron. Like a great bell it was. They heard the soup go slosh into his bowl. They heard him sipping at his spoon. And the ones nearest the door heard the soup gurgling in his belly.

Still they sat.

They heard the sound of sausages sizzling in the pan. They smelt the sausages. They saw the smoke coming under the door, and the ones nearest the door even heard him sprinkling salt and pepper on them.

Still they sat.

They heard the sound of a knife cutting cake, the crack of the icing and the swish through cream. They heard him smacking his lips and licking his fingers, and the ones nearest the door even heard him picking up crumbs.

> Eat a bit
> Tim Tom Tackler
> Eat a bit
> Tackler Tom.

The people in the hall were going mad with hunger. What was the king up to?

Just when it seemed as if everyone was going to burst, the king spoke to the guards.

"Guards! Open the doors!"

Then he turned to the court and spoke again. "You may go," he said.

Like a great fierce dragon they rushed out of the hall, down the steps, round the corner and into the kitchen where the boy was finishing his dinner. And, like one fierce dragon, they leapt on the boy and pulled him apart.

"Dinner, dinner, dinner," some shouted.

"Drink, drink, drink," others shouted.

Upstairs the king waited.

Soon his court came rushing back.

"We got him," some shouted. "We did for him!"

And then the king who never chopped anyone's head off spoke.

"The next person to make a noise will die."

This time everyone did as they were told and they all went very quiet.

When I first read "The King Who Promised" by Michael Rosen, it did not strike me as extraordinary. I should explain why it was an unlikely choice for me, to make clear that my objections are purely personal ones; it may well be the ideal story for somebody else. First, I think I have a lot of maturing to do as a storyteller before I will find myself inclined to tell a story which transmits such a deeply disturbing message about the human psyche. For me, the proven fact that when evil is in power it can cause ordinary people to commit horrifyingly cruel acts is the most frightening thing I can think of. I prefer to turn my cowardly back on such knowledge. If I were more politically sophisticated, perhaps I would want to tell this story in the realization that there is a battle to be waged, always, against such forces — against autocrats with false promises — and that the stories of the ones who fight are the most uplifting of all. Their stories provide the true counter-melody to the discord of destructive power, at least for those with more optimism than I have.

In a way, the harmony of this tale is audible in Tim Tom Tackler's song: the singing kitchen lad remains merrily himself to the bitter end. Herein, in fact, lies enormous scope for a different kind of storyteller from me — the grown-up clown sort. Michael Rosen himself, a superb professional performer, is such a one. Even in the days when I hardly knew my step-son-to-be, when he was being most careful to draw me, the newcomer, into the Rosen ring, one method of induction was to grab me in a bear-hug and make subdued snuffling, squelchy noises in the nape of my neck, intended to sound like a catarrhal nose-blow. Michael, his brother and, indeed, his father would relish the leaping and laughing of the little kitchen boy and all the noises he is responsible for — the bangings, sloshings, sippings, gurglings, sizzlings, tricklings, swishings, smackings, lickings . . . Oh yes, for some, "The King Who Promised" would be a very sound choice indeed! But for me it wasn't the same cup of tea as "The Land Where No One Ever Dies" proved to be (see pages 93-96).

I am quite sure that all of us launching into storytelling for the first time should trust our own instincts about which stories to choose (assuming we also have an instinct for what will go down well with children!) and stick to that instinct for some time, irrespective of fitting it around a particular theme, scheme or project. There are thousands of stories readily available everywhere, so what we choose is neither here nor there. Then we discover that we can make what we want of almost any story — just as children do, without any apparent inhibition, fortunately for English teachers!

I may not have admired "The King . . ." but I immediately recognized it as *useful* material and that, as my husband would say, was "a different gether altomatter." I have included it because it was instrumental in causing a major change in my attitude to storytelling and retelling, as I discovered in 1/T.

■ THE 1/T CLASS

As far as story-hearing was concerned, 1/T was a difficult class, or so I thought. I couldn't help comparing it with its companion class 1/U. In 1/U a communal spirit accentuated the individuality of its members because the contribution each made, whether in dialogue or in presenting a piece of original composition, emerged within an atmosphere of acceptance and respect. Each individual, therefore, had the space to become more intensely himself. Simultaneously, however, by its very nature the group built up a store of shared attitudes and behaviours, very often directed, moulded and extended by me, and together amalgamating into a durable, mutually acceptable social order. I would like to think that such experience was a training for life; that when the 1/U group dispersed and the individuals became party to very different communities — of workers, of neighbours, of local, regional and world citizens — such caring principles remained with them. But that may be so much wishful thinking.

It was not wishful thinking in the classroom, but an everyday fact. I cannot exaggerate the effect on me of lessons with such groups. They made me believe that if my preparation was right, then nothing could go wrong. At the outset of every new venture, whether it was a large scheme of work or just the reading of a poem or the telling of a tale, there was always that tickle of excitement: something uniquely new was about to occur. There would be productivity. And within the familiarity of civilized sharing, amazing individual differences would sprout. Of course sometimes things did go wrong and lessons were decidedly less than perfect, but that underlying sense of security and the promise of good things just round the corner never went.

I am immediately reminded of an occasion from a more youthful era when I used to fish. The best day I ever had was in the Lake District when I worked my way along a little Tennyson-type stream until it turned into quite a powerful river. Though I felt certain that a fat trout lurked behind every boulder, in the spread reflection of each bankside tree, and particularly in the smooth pool at the base of every waterfall, I caught absolutely nothing. But the glorious excitement of anticipation did not abate, even while I stole some of my precious fishing time to rummage in my rucksack for marie biscuits, a lump of oily rock-hard Cheddar, crumbly fruit cake and a pound of cooking apples covered with little round declivities and bruisy brown bits — a great meal!

Such was the anticipation and realization of achievement with 1/U, but 1/T was different in two very important respects. First, it was a collection of individuals who were quite disparate in temperament. They made isolated but tenuous friendships, in pairs and one threesome, but there was nothing of the whole-group gelling which for me literally characterized 1/U and most other classes I taught at that school. This was a significant disadvantage both to the class and to me.

My plans for my very first lesson with 1/T were abandoned halfway through when someone made an anti-semitic remark. Such moments had taught me how to pursue issues quietly and patiently while in fact seething inside. Well into the chat that followed when someone insisted that Jews were miserly, I casually threw in that I knew that couldn't be so because I was married to a Jew and he was as generous a person as anyone I'd ever met. I had already decided that the next lesson — or as near to it as he could manage — I would have my husband in to talk to them about his Jewish childhood in the East End. In all sorts of ways I sought to extend the sympathies and tolerances of what was in fact a quite jolly group of children who were actually very warmly disposed towards the teacher who now sounds so denigratory; but, alas, they never quite learned mutual warmth. Little spites, a mocking guffaw, a nasty jibe, accusations, relevant or not to the matter in hand, squirted out every now and again. In this way the most adventurous, speculative and subtle intimations of each one's individuality were often suppressed. I was never totally relaxed with them, because even during the very good moments — which were frequent — I had a sense that there was an element of containment in what was on the surface a beautiful relationship!

The second major difference distinguishing 1/T not just from 1/U but from all my classes at that time was that it was not genuine mixed-ability but relatively much lower in conventional attainment terms — which presented obvious problems to me as their English teacher. But what was even more frustrating was that it seemed a class without the sparkle I was used to, although it was not lacking in energy.

What I am saying is that there were two good reasons why telling stories to 1/T wouldn't work: the pupils didn't get on well together and, to put it crudely, they were not very bright. The event was quite unexpectedly different from the theory, however. These "two good reasons" crumbled to dust. First, though an in-built collaborative attitude was not a feature of 1/T, it turned out that the special sense of anticipation created quite simply by a gathering together for the "Once upon a time" experience was enough to sink all antagonisms and create an essential — albeit short-lived — harmony. Could it be, I have asked myself since, that an accumulation of such experiences would have made permanent and real that temporary unity? Secondly, the effect of listening to the story was such that the ensuing individual work by the pupils was of a much higher standard than they generally achieved. These were most important discoveries for me as a secondary English teacher, with far-reaching implications regarding the educational significance of story retelling in the curriculum.

But it was not until June of that academic year that I discovered all this. Because of the "two good reasons," I had not fancied launching into storytelling with 1/T, which was a shame. When it did occur my motives were quite different from what they had been in the story group or with 1/U or 2/C. My year with 1/T was almost done and demands were coming in from on high for *marks* and *grades*. I was anxious to set some task which involved as substantial a piece of writing as each could muster and which would enable me to get a realistic picture of their technical skills in written English on a comparative basis. It needed to be something that involved their using at least a common vocabulary. No doubt on that one occasion I could have provided something really old-fashioned like a dictation, but I need hardly describe the pitfalls of such an exercise with such a group; quite apart from that, people do best when their hearts are involved! I decided to tell them a story, one simple enough for them to take in but intriguing enough to turn them all on. My choice was the Michael Rosen story I had already noted as useful.

I gave them some indication of what my purposes were, though I stressed that I wanted to discover how well they could remember, rather than spell and punctuate, the words I would use. Then I retold Michael's story. I had not reread it beforehand; therefore my telling contained some details that don't appear in the original and omitted some that do. Some of these changes are obvious from recurring bits in the children's work reproduced below.

On this occasion, for obvious reasons, I asked them to keep as close as possible in their retellings to how I had told it, explaining that this was not in any way "original" writing. So much for theory again. In practice it is simply not possible to demand that an act of listening be totally receptive. It would seem that listening is interpreting is creating. Thought is free, praise be!

Let me begin with a complete and exact retelling by one of the "technically" weakest of this group of mixed but generally low attainers.

■ MARK'S STORY

Once a promise was made by a noble king how was a grate leader he ruled many lands. The king stood up one day in the dining hall and made a promised. he promised that he would not chop peoples head or kill his subjects in any way at all. The people were joyfull so joyfull that every one of his subjects jumped for joy they sang and talked out louid. this made the king angry and angry suddenly a volcano burst in his stomerk. he said "silnce" out louid so Louid everybody in the place herd him then every one stord silint except one boy a kitchen boy he stord sing out louid every one in the dinning room Looked at him the king got a key and went over to the big oak doors a put the boy in the kitchen a locked the door. but the boy kept on singing then everybody herd a clang then more clanging of pots and pans and a smell of meat a soup a other good things. Then a banging of a spoon hitting the side of a caulderon. then a surplin of soup and a choping of meat, OH the people were angry and angry and so was the king. The king said "go into the kitchen" and every body waited outside the doors then the king opened the doors. All the angry people rushed inside and tore the boy lim from lim. then they had the rest off the soup and meat. They were so happy that everybody had to sing and laugh again. Then the king said "silince you can see what people can do using other people". the people fought [thought] for a moment a realised how stupid they were and learned a lesson.

Some might say: "Come, come! This is no illiterate twelve-year-old. Plenty of children are far weaker." And I would agree. Though the writer is more fluent here than usual, certainly the weakest in l/T wrote substantially less, in a way that the impatient or uninitiated would describe as unreadable. Others might say: "What a mess! Look at the spelling and punctuation!" (Some people only see things like that when pupils write.) And I would reply that if a child writes consistently with commitment and energy, this spelling and punctuation weakness is easy to remedy given time, and not much time either. It was the story that won him over, and more where that one came from went on to effect very acceptable changes in his level of "correctness." And look at the achievement! Here is a totally clear, sequential retelling; pleasing internal rhythms occur in the opening lines and beyond; the writer's representation of uncorked fury as "suddenly a volcano burst in his stomach" is his own poetry, worth a moment of anyone's attention; and what's more, surprisingly, in inventing the king's final pronouncement he reveals an insight into the story's message which dawned on seventeen-year-old Lennie, in another class, only after several minutes of to-ing and fro-ing with his teacher all to himself. This is an intelligent retelling. It could be called a "comprehension," could it not?

■ OTHER STORIES

What follows is a little something from others in the group. With the technical errors removed, it might prove impossible to divide the sheep from the goats in conventional school terms. Which isn't at all surprising, especially in written work that follows on from a storytelling. The very least that was revealed in every child who heard the story that day was a capacity to produce clear "complex" sentences in writing, without assistance, something which had not been much in evidence up to that point in the least able members of the class, represented here:

The king was furious so he locked the boy up in the kitchen and there was total silence in the court room.

The big doors swung open and the young kitchen boy who had stopped singing asked them in and they ate till their bellies were full.

The remains of the boy were scattered on the floor and that's what happens to somebody who disobeys a king.

Many children flexed their linguistic muscles and achieved an impressive tone:

There once lived a king who had a promise to make to his people, so the king led his people into the royal court . . .   The king on the royal throne was frowning again — he was angry but he just refused to show it for he wanted to see . . .

He called the subjects of his court to proclaim this promise . . .   This made
the courtiers extremely envious of the kitchen boy . . .   The king read their
thoughts and smiled to himself wickedly.

Literature, we all believe, extends the sensibilities. This story homed
directly in on the pupils' sympathetic nerve, which responded to the lot of
the oppressed:

The king stood up so fast with a big clash that made them all jump. He made
others bring up their food to their throat. But in the kitchen lay the remains
of the little cook. He must have been stepped on, pushed around and kicked.
The poor little cook was lying on the floor opposite the big cauldron.

But slowly the boy died of shock, of terror.

They ran into the kitchen and hit the boy. When they had finished with the
boy they flung him on the ground, they rushed to the eating of all the left-over
meat and drinking down the soup. But the kitchen boy was lying, not singing.

People were sad about the broken promise and remembered him, the singer.

Most significant of all was the eagerness with which each child
got down to it. Their imaginations sang along:

Slowly the king took the golden bright key out of his robe, the robe with the
silver star on.

A few minutes later singing came from the keyhole and after that m m
m m slurp slurp! Everybody's mouth watered. They wondered how the soup
tasted. Not too soon the people could hear the kitchen boy grinding his meat
and the last a a a a giving the sign of pleasure . . .
    The men of the court felt angry that the boy was eating — and here I am
with a hungry stomach!
    The king took out the key that matched the doors. He stepped forward
to the door. You could hear the king's footsteps echoing.

The differences in the pupils' mental pictures threw to the four winds
my request that they stick closely to the words I had used. In order to show
this extraordinary variety of vision, I have restricted the following extracts
to one portion of the story only: the point where the king first demands
silence.

    The noise started to rise and rise and the king was not very happy that
there was a lot of noise because he didn't like noise very much. Even then one
person shouted, a young kitchen boy who worked in the kitchen next to the
great court. It had great oak doors and when the banquet came the great oak

tables would be taken out and the silver salver and lid cover. Then the king raised his voice and said silence in court and not a sound was made except that the kitchen boy kept singing and singing. Then the king raised his voice again and said go in the kitchen so the boy did.

There was a lot of noise. Some people even sang. The king was getting very irritated by this after a while so he said, "Let there be no noise!" Everyone stopped when he said this — they were scared even though he had promised not to chop anyone's head off. All was silent — well, nearly all. A small kitchen boy was still singing. The king was very angry. The people were very surprised. The king said, "Go into the kitchen." With that, the boy smiled and walked into the kitchen.

Everyone was laughing and the noise level grew so high that the king was getting irritable and shouted "Silence in Court" so everyone was scared and stopped except for one small boy who was still singing with joy.

The king was on his throne but the sound went higher and higher until the king could not take the sound anymore. The king shouted, "Let there be SILENCE! IN! THE! COURT!" At once everybody was quiet, not a sound from anyone. They all stared at the king. There was a sound of singing. It was a kitchen boy. Everybody turned and looked. He was singing and dancing. "A BOY," shouted the king, "A BOY!"

There was a sudden hush and then everybody started to laugh and the king got angry and more angry and he said "Quiet!" then everybody went quiet except the kitchen boy. He was still singing to himself.

The people laugh louder, louder, loud as they can. They sang happily. Everybody was happy in the palace except the king who was angry in his heart and his heart got more angry and more angry in his heart. Then he roars as hard as he can. He made the court into silence. That was a sign of relief — he would not change his mind. But suddenly a boy from the palace in the royal kitchen was cooking the king's dinner and the royal guests' dinner. But he sang a song. The king couldn't roar his heart because his heart was soft like a feather. The king called to the boy, "Stop, please stop! At once!" but the boy didn't stop.

The people were giggling and pushing each other. Then a noise came from the kitchen. It was the kitchen boy. He was singing. The king called to the boy in the kitchen. When the boy came out the king said to the boy, "Go back in the kitchen and close the door in silence."

The king got very irritated because the noise level was so high, then shouted "Silence." Upon this order everyone became silent on that instance except a little kitchen boy who was still singing. The king was irritated because he wanted to chop his head off but he remembered his promise. Then he ordered the little boy into the kitchen and slammed the two big wooden doors shut and put the key into the inside pocket of his scarlet robe.

The people were happy. They were singing, cheering, happy — hoora, hoora, hoora! They were cheering like mad and loud, loud, loud! But the king said "Be quiet or I shall get somebody to execute you." The people were silent but a boy was singing.

The king was getting a bit angry with the level of the noise. He began to frown. Then with his mighty voice he shouted, "Let there be silence!" Everyone hushed. They looked at the king in a funny way. The king spoke again. "I know I have made a promise that I won't chop nobody's head off but still you don't have to shout and scream." There was silence now. The big wooden arched doors opened. You could see the kitchen and the servants and the maids. They all entered the court. There was one little cook, a very young boy who came in singing. Everyone except this little boy was silent. The king was again upset because the boy did not obey his king. He was sent back to the kitchen. The doors shut again. From the keyhole was heard the little boy's voice. Everybody stood listening to the boy singing. But something else came through the keyhole. There was an aroma, the smell of spices in soup drifting through the air.

All these pieces catch the flavour of traditional narration. There were two exceptions. Here is the same portion of the story in the very different register of an adult who had a sophisticated literary background. She, amongst others in a group of teachers and the like, after listening to the opening of the story, was given the bare facts of what followed and asked to turn them into a continuation of the living, breathing tale.

The people cheered and applauded this statement. The king smiled in a fatherly way at first then, as the noise continued, and the audience failed to notice his obvious signs of distress at the abnormal noise, he called for quiet. The noise gradually subsided. A little kitchen boy, however, continued to sing out loud and clear. The king ordered his arrest and removed him from the hall. He was locked out. The others were thereby locked in.

This uncomfortably formal prose — "applauded this statement," "failed to notice his obvious signs of distress," "abnormal noise," "gradually subsided" and, horror of horrors, "thereby" — is a total disaster beside the efforts of 1/T. The writer was a participant in "A Telling Exchange," the 17th Conference on Language in Inner City Schools held at the University of London Institute of Education in July 1984. She was modest enough to proffer this judgement for herself and kind enough to let me quote what she had written as an example of how the trained English teacher can sometimes lose where children instinctively win.

There was one, and only one, child in 1/T who failed to catch a storyteller's voice, though in quite a different way:

> The noise got so loud the king got a very bad headache and he began to get furious. He told all the people to be quiet and they all shut up except the little kitchen boy so the king told the boy to shut up but he kept on singing so the king put the boy into the kitchen and locked the big wooden doors and put the key in the left side of his robe and then there was complete silence . . .

The writer had come late to the lesson, the delay caused by an official investigation into some misdemeanour the nature of which it is probably as well I have forgotten. The fact that he missed the opening bit of the tale does not explain his rather bleak chain of facts and the jarring "shut up," since I provided him with his own personal telling in whispers while the rest of the class got on with the writing. The explanation lies elsewhere. Within this rather anti-social group this particular boy had, if I dare say it, the hardest of hearts. When he arrived on the scene that day he was at first disconcerted by the absorbed atmosphere in the room and then decidedly aggrieved to be deprived of a fully flamboyant entry on account of the hissing "sshhh's" from his colleagues. Revenge seemed sweetly on the cards with his smug announcement: "I can't do the writing, miss, coz I wasn't here!" But as I said, I thwarted that one. What he lacked was the anonymity of listening to the story with the others. It was some way into my whispered telling that I observed his eyes and mouth gradually, reluctantly shed his determination to keep his distance — but it was too late.

It is the mean spirit, not the low achiever, who is hardest to woo. He heard the whole of the story; what he missed was the creative receptivity of a community of listeners, a chance to lay aside his egocentricity while compassed about with a cloud of witnesses. On the other hand, that useful tale got him down to the writing unobtrusively and without serious demur, which was unique for him. And in later discussion his classmates spotted the "shut up," so he learned something in literary, if not in moral, terms!

■ LENNIE

That same year I was teaching Lennie, a 5. He was a tall, gangling Trinidadian who usually smiled broadly, but who was also given to frighteningly smouldering sulks which I knew, from having taught him two years earlier, were founded in the fact that he never enjoyed the feeling of success. The best and the most he was able to achieve during that year, in the bottom group, was the following piece of writing (spelling mistakes doctored by me):

THE BAD SIDE OF HAVING A BROTHER OR SISTER

If you take him to school and he runs in the road they will put the blame on to you because you are the old one. You look out — they must not run on the road. The bad side of having a brother or sister is suppose I am looking at TV and my brother or sisters come into the room and turn it off and I put it back on my brother will go and tell my dad that I put on the TV.

They are too fussy. Suppose my brother tells my dad that my bed is untidy and my dad tells me to make it up and I say "his bed is untidy too" so he will tell him to make it up then my brother will say it is not fair. He will make funny faces at you and call you names.

That's what I don't like about the bad side of brothers and sisters.

Now, two years later, he was in a mixed-ability class as everyone had been, for English lessons, since the beginning of the previous academic year, when we had got rid of streaming for good. Unfortunately it happened to be the most difficult of the 5's, chock-a-block not just with smoulderers but with active firebrands who, for most of the year, simply couldn't accept that English Language, designed for the bulk of the pupils, was the least bit worth the bother.

Lennie demanded hours of patience, not simply because he stood a chance of rising high enough for a lowest level pass (rather than remaining "unclassified" or "not entered," which happened in all his other subjects except woodwork), but because he needed desperately every possible boost to his minuscule morale. He knew that almost every demand made in school classrooms would be too much for him. All his classmates knew this too, but such is the nature of the Tottenham beast that their attitude to him was totally good-natured — and more, as it turned out. By February, when most of the group were beginning to get their English Language Examination act together (though no one would openly admit as much), Lennie quite suddenly hit his lowest ebb. He put his head in his hands and cried at his desk, solidly and unstoppably. I sat next to him, questioning, being silent, persuading, being silent, comforting, being silent. This lasted for about an hour, right up to the end of the lesson, and incredibly, all the while, that permanently rowdy class withdrew into itself and, with no directive from me, got on with work that each individual member set for himself, without a sound in the room to accompany Lennie's subdued sobbing. If ever I should teach in a different school it will have to be in an ethnically mixed working class area with London West Indian kids predominating!

He heaved himself out of the room at the first sound of the bell, and I assumed that Lennie and English were through. What had finally thrown him at the start of that miserable lesson was the most intimidating portion of the evaluation performance folder, the one requiring book reviews. Read a book? The most Lennie had read on his own in the way of literature was one or two of Michael Rosen's shortest poems, so conveniently simple in language but so wonderfully perceptive in content, about the rivalries and revelries of brothers. Lennie read a book? He knew he hadn't a hope. While he had wept and I had sat with my arm going numb over his seventeen-year-old shoulders, I had assured him that of course he could finish his folder and that by the very next lesson I would find "books" he would be able to read. Ah well, that was that — or so I thought until the next day when suddenly Lennie was at my door, full of unsolicited apologies, his smile sheepish rather than its usual massive.

That was when, quick as a flash, we got down to work armed with "The King Who Promised," in book form. Lennie was not alone in being conned by the ambience of the opening sentence. The whole story had been put into a merry little paperback: two or three lines of print per page with easy-to-read, repetitively constructed sentences; the inside laced with chirpy, slick sketches and the outside with a blandly smiling king lounging in his crown, his cloak (a collage of bits of *The Times* newspaper's Court Circular column . . . odd, but hardly noticeable on first glance) and gorgeously jolly, long-leggedy striped trousers, with his thumbs and toes pointing jauntily upwards. And what have you got but the ideal item for a fond mummy with a quid to spare to take home for junior? Not that it mattered in our local children's bookshop owner. While the adults of her world may well find her dogmatic statements rather intimidating, children are treated royally — she knows the contents of every book on her copious shelves and no young clients could be better served. She refused to stock "The King Who Promised" — at least she did in 1976 when it was published in the form I have described.

After I'd read it with Lennie there was a lot of to-ing and fro-ing to prove the point, but he was finally happy to go away and write his own version of the story and what he thought of it. That was his first taste of book reviews.

Eventually, after the long post-exam wait during which I worried more about him than any of the high "O" level candidates, Lennie qualified in English. He was so enormously pleased that he made several visits to the school to remind me of it for some time after he had left.

And I learned, once and for all, that story retelling in the classroom is a powerful and neglected source of achievement for pupils. And teachers! And that I can still relish the telling of a story in spite of its not having much appeal as far as I personally am concerned. That's what I mean by useful material.

Five

SELECTING AND PREPARING MATERIAL FOR STORYTELLING

After the success of "The King Who Promised" with 1/T I continued to tell stories to my classes, though not as frequently or in as planned a manner as I now know I should have done. My attention was focused upon the effects of a rude shift I found myself obliged to make from teaching a cross-section of age groups to teaching the older pupils exclusively — the 4's (14-15 years) to the 6's (16-18 years). Among the massive demands of examination coursework there was no obvious slot for oral stories, and I regret to say it was some time before I was moved to make the necessary space. But, inspired by the memory of my younger pupils' achievement, I did enough to realize that I could make what I wanted of a story. I could mould and modify original material enough to my own taste and purposes. It is this process I want to consider here.

Luckily I had become aware of the growing interest in narrative, both as an academic study and as exemplified in the number of professional and semi-professional storytellers about. This growing interest was important, too, for members of minority groups in our cities, whose contribution to British culture would certainly include a wealth of "new" tales, deserving of proper recognition. Inevitably I met other teachers with the same awarenesses. Almost by accident I found myself telling the story of Orpheus to a group of teachers and lecturers (a much larger group than I had expected) as the starting point of a workshop on narrative run by my husband. This rash move resulted in fellow teachers coming to me afterwards as though I was a real storyteller, some kind of expert or gifted creature with mystiques duly attached! However, I shall describe here not *the* way to learn to tell stories but *one* way: the route *I* followed. And if I learned, then any teacher who simply wants to have a go can do so.

I'll begin by recalling the words of two strangers, who later became friends in collaborative work on narrative in the school setting:

"How do you learn to tell stories, then?"

"I'd never told them a story before but after a few sentences of the Orpheus story the kids were listening with more attention than they'd ever done before!"

The question and the statement came to me during different meetings of the London Narrative Group, which consisted of teachers who had joined together soon after that narrative workshop to share different versions of narrative in the classroom. Both had heard me tell the story of Orpheus and Eurydice at a Language in the Inner City Conference, so my *unspoken* reactions were swift: to the first, "There's nothing to it!"; to the second, "There — I told you so!"

In this chapter I shall take up the challenge of the question. I take it up as an English teacher, not as a professional storyteller, nor even as an English teacher whose forte is telling stories. Just as an English teacher. There is no doubt that there is such a category as the "born" storyteller, but if, like me, you are not a natural in the field, then let me share my lesson preparation with you.

Here is the basic foursome:

- Find a story you like massively; a story your imagination will relish, cherish and nourish.

- Get all the facts and details together, even those you will later reject: there's a lot of lesson preparation involved, although, with luck, your pupils will never guess!

- Decide what you are going to include, note it down in sequence and, in the process, consider particularly carefully how you are going to begin.

- Visualize the start precisely; by this I mean allow the opening situation to occupy — take over — your imagination. This will go a long way towards ensuring that you will speak with your own voice a story that has become your own.

You may have a favourite story from childhood days which has always haunted you; or you may happen upon one which grabs you; or you may satisfactorily complete a conscious search through storybooks for *the* one to launch you into this particular classroom activity. If so, that takes care of the first step and probably the second as well, in which case you may want to skip what is written below and move to the third part of the process.

Essentially the story must become your own before you retell it, "revisioned" by you so that your reception of it becomes a complete creative act. This is not so unlikely a possibility if you ponder the fact that reading itself is thought by many to be a creative, as opposed to a passive, process.

I will take you through my process, using as an example the story of Demeter and Persephone. But first some extracts from Robert Graves's *The Greek Myths.*

■ DEMETER

Though the priestesses of Demeter, goddess of the cornfield, initiate brides and bridegrooms into the secrets of the couch, she has no husband of her own. While still young and gay, she bore Core and the lusty Iachus to Zeus, her brother, out of wedlock. She also bore Plutus to the Titan Iasius, or Iasion, with whom she fell in love at the wedding of Cadmus and Harmonia . . .

Demeter herself has a gentle soul and Erysichthon, son of Tropias, was one of the few men with whom she ever dealt harshly. At the head of twenty companions, Erysichthon dared invade a grove which the Pelasgians had planted for her at Dotium, and began cutting down the sacred trees . . .

Demeter lost her gaiety for ever when young Core, afterwards called Persephone, was taken from her. Hades fell in love with Core, and went to ask Zeus's leave to marry her. Zeus feared to offend his eldest brother by a downright refusal, but knew also that Demeter would not forgive him if Core were committed to Tartarus; he therefore answered politically that he could neither give nor withhold his consent. This emboldened Hades to abduct the girl, as she was picking flowers in a meadow — it may have been at Sicilian Enna . . . She sought Core without rest for nine days and nights, neither eating nor drinking, and calling fruitlessly all the while. The only news she could get came from old Hecate, who early one morning had heard Core crying "A rape! A rape!" but, on hurrying to the rescue, found no sign of her.

On the tenth day, after a disagreeable encounter with Poseidon among the herds of Oncus, Demeter came in disguise . . .

For Triptolemus, who herded his father's cattle, had recognized Demeter and given her the news she needed: ten days before this his brothers Eumolpus, a shepherd, and Eubuleus, a swineherd, had been out in the fields, feeding their beasts, when the earth suddenly gaped open, engulfing Eubuleus's swine before his very eyes; then, with a heavy thud of hooves, a chariot drawn by black horses appeared, and dashed down the chasm. The chariot-driver's face was invisible, but his right arm was tightly clasped around a shrieking girl. Eumolpus had been told of the event by Eubuleus, and made it the subject of a lament.

Armed with this evidence, Demeter summoned Hecate. Together they approached Helius, who sees everything, and forced him to admit that Hades had been the villain, doubtless with the connivance of his brother Zeus. Demeter was so angry that, instead of returning to Olympus, she continued to wander the earth, forbidding the trees to yield fruit and the herbs to grow, until the race of men stood in danger of extinction. Zeus, ashamed to visit Demeter in person at Eleusis, sent her first a message by Iris . . . But she would not return to Olympus, and swore that the earth must remain barren until Core had been restored.

Only one course of action remained for Zeus. He sent Hermes with a message to Hades: "If you do not restore Core, we are all undone!" and with another to Demeter: "You may have your daughter again, on the single condition that she has not yet tasted the food of the dead."

Because Core had refused to eat so much as a crust of bread ever since her abduction, Hades was obliged to cloak his vexation, telling her mildly: "My child, you seem to be unhappy here, and your mother weeps for you. I have therefore decided to send you home."

Core's tears ceased to flow, and Hermes helped her to mount his chariot. But, just as she was setting off for Eleusis, one of Hades's gardeners, by name Ascalaphus, began to cry and hoot derisively. "Having seen the Lady Core," he said, "pick a pomegranate from a tree in your orchard, and eat seven seeds, I am ready to bear witness that she has tasted the food of the dead!" Hades grinned, and told Ascalaphus to perch on the back of Hermes's chariot.

At Eleusis, Demeter joyfully embraced Core; but, on hearing about the pomegranate seeds, grew more dejected than ever, and said again, "I will neither return to Olympus, nor remove my curse from the land." Zeus then persuaded Rhea, the mother of Hades, Demeter, and himself, to plead with her; and a compromise was at last reached. Core should spend three months of the year in Hades's company, as Queen of Tartarus, with the title of Persephone, and the remaining nine months in Demeter's. Hecate offered to make sure that this arrangement was kept, and to keep constant watch on Core.

Demeter finally consented to return home. Before leaving Eleusis, she instructed Triptolemus, Eumolpus, and Celeus . . . in her worship and mysteries. But she punished Ascalaphus for his tale-bearing . . .

Triptolemus she supplied with seed-corn, a wooden plough, and a chariot drawn by serpents . . .

All this does not exactly skip along! *The Greek Myths* is very much a reference book rather than a convenient collection of short stories, but it became my bible for a series of storytelling lessons.

■ MAKING THE CHOICE

Since the Orpheus myth has always enchanted me, I planned to make it the climax of the series. This meant I had to create the Underworld for the boys as a recognizable landscape, peopled with souls whom they would expect Orpheus to meet and influence. So I prepared and subsequently told the histories of Ixion, Tantalus, Sisyphus, Charon, Cerberus and Persephone.

The most productive tales turned out to be the ones I deeply liked myself, rather than those I told simply to fit into Orpheus's journey. The story of Tantalus, in addition to magic, wonder and a climax of unending punishment, had a fair bit of humour. And I loved the story of Persephone, Demeter and Hades, where some of the appeal is instantly obvious even in the briefest outline:

Demeter was the goddess of agriculture. Her daughter Persephone was carried off by Hades to the Underworld. Demeter refused to let any crops grow until Persephone was brought back. It was finally agreed that Persephone should spend eight months with Demeter and four with Hades.

From *Greek Myths*, Macdonalds Junior Reference Library

(I'm not proud!)

Inevitably a story which explains one of the most amazing wonders of the earth — seasonal growth, fruition, death and rebirth — has enormous appeal. Add to this the beginning of the story as told in the *Encyclopaedia Britannica:*

Persephone is the consort of Hades who carried her off while she was gathering flowers.

The story touches on romantic love (incidentally a nice precursor to the far more moving love between Orpheus and Eurydice), the poignancy of parting, and the yearning for a lost one (again, aptly close to what was to be the climax of a term's work), but what most appealed to me is its base — which is the love between mother and child — and its portrayal of their mutual longing for each other, to infinity.

Yet it is not enough to find a story which is personally appealing; it also has to be right for the pupils. This one would be, I was sure. In addition, it offered the opportunity in my all-male classroom for follow-up work involving some anti-sexist insights into motherhood.

■ COLLECTING THE DETAIL

As I have already indicated, this story had to be pieced together for my own purposes from a variety of sources. A purist, no doubt, would have explored all Robert Graves's references, but there's a limit to the hours available to a full-time classroom teacher! There was more than enough for me in his section "Demeter's Nature and Deeds."

I retained the main thread of the story but named only the chief characters. Other than Zeus (known to my pupils from the tales I had already told them), the only names were Helius and Hecate, whom I included partly because I thought their roles quite intriguing and also because some of the boys would meet Hecate fleetingly when they read *Macbeth* a year later in the fifth form: such tie-ups can be satisfying. I reduced the peopling of Demeter's wanderings simply to her meeting with the shepherd Eumolpus in his father's house, but without naming either. I felt Hades' bargaining with Zeus and the business of the pomegranate seeds was enough in the way of relevant complexity.

For this kind of selection I suppose each storyteller has to consciously test out all the parts of the whole to see how much fits easily together within his or her purposes and ranges as a teller of that particular story. My aim is always to establish and sustain the tone of a story, which is why I think the first steps of the process are so critical for me.

■ FINDING THE STARTING POINT

The story of Demeter and her daughter is profoundly about birth, nurture, loss and renewal. And, at the risk of sounding pretentious, I wanted my telling to give a sense of the rich cycle of the earth and its progeny. Does that seem a far cry from the ambience of a classroom full of tough, multi-ethnic fifteen-year-old lads who hail from the environs of the Broadwater Farm Estate, Tottenham? Don't you believe it! On this occasion I got as close as I was able to what I intended in the telling, and they responded with an absorbed stillness which put me in mind of Wordsworth's nun, "breathless with adoration." I mean for the words, of course, not for the speaker!

So — to the first critical sentences. The words of that London group member are apt: if the beginning takes hold of the listeners, then there'll be no bubble gum poppings, chair tippings, key rattlings or the like until the tale is told, and even then it will be necessary for them to remind each other of who they are. Here were the possibilities I considered from Graves's text.

- Demeter, goddess of the cornfield . . . has no husband of her own. While still young and gay, she bore Core . . . to Zeus, her brother, out of wedlock.

A promising start. I was anxious not to exclude paternal concern from the story. In fact in my telling I softened the Zeus of the text by allowing him a good deal of anxiety over Persephone's welfare. But I did not feel that an opening reference to the fathering of his sister's child was quite the right means of soothing my charges into silence!

■ Demeter herself has a gentle soul . . . lost her gaiety forever when young
  Core . . . was taken from her.

This I quite liked. I could get my mind around such a starter:

Demeter, goddess of summer's harvest, was a gentle woman who loved all young
plants and all the fruits and seeds that flourish in the good earth. But there
was one young creature whom she loved above all else, and that was her only
daughter, Persephone. What horror and pain were in store for her, then, when
Hades, powerful god of the Underworld, where little grows in the half light,
fell in love with her daughter . . .

Well, maybe not: maybe Lee or Leroy would find that a bit soppy,
although later on in the story they'd lap it up.

■ Hades fell in love with Core, and went to ask Zeus's leave to marry her.
  Zeus feared to offend his eldest brother by a downright refusal, but knew
  also that Demeter would not forgive him if Core were committed to
  Tartarus.

This focus on Hades' negotiations with Zeus is background information
to the main events, and I felt it might be a bit cold-blooded for the
beginning; it could come in incidentally at some point. I didn't want to put
any initial emphasis on Hades' viewpoint either.

■ This emboldened Hades to abduct the girl, as she was picking flowers in
  a meadow.

Irresistible!

So precious was Persephone to her mother, the godess Demeter, that it was rare
for her to be out alone, and even then Persephone was careful to return home
before the sun had set for she knew how anxious her mother would become,
and loved her the more for that. But one drowsy afternoon she forgot about
time passing. She had been gathering wild flowers, for, like her mother, she loved
the blossoms of the field and meadowland. Just as the sun rested on the horizon,
she spotted a patch of yellow cowslips some distance away . . .

Oh yes, I could get really carried away with that one, perhaps incorporating a tincture of botanical description (my inner-city pupils would not
be over-familiar with cowslips), or maybe I'd steal a word or two from
"Where the bee sucks." On the other hand, one must not forget Lee and
Leroy, not to mention Ricky's group who always gaggle together, even when
the class is sitting round me for the story rather than at their desks. It had
better come later.

- The only news she could get came from old Hecate, who early one morning had heard Core crying "A rape! A rape!" but, on hurrying to the rescue, found no sign of her.

This could be quite dramatic. I would make it dusk rather than dawn. And I'd get rid of Core's words since it was story studies, not social studies.

As darkness fell, old Hecate, alone with her cauldron of spells, heard a shrill cry of distress before it was carried away by the warm south wind. It was the shriek of a young girl, full of fear. Hecate knew that voice: it was surely the voice of the precious daughter of Demeter, goddess of the corn, the harvest; goddess of the rich fruits of the earth. Hecate took up a flaming torch and went to search the darkness, but she searched in vain . . .

Possible.

- [He sent a message] to Demeter: "You may have your daughter again, on the single condition that she has not yet tasted the food of the dead."

Here was a good bit of traditional magic: shades of the forbidden fruit, the label "Drink me," Snow White's near fatal bite, the apples of youth in the Baba Yaga story I'd told 4/C when they were in the second year. But the tone wasn't quite right for the main theme, so this episode would have to wait for its appointed place in the chronology.

- Eumolpus, a shepherd, and Eubuleus, a swineherd, had been out in the fields, feeding their beasts, when the earth suddenly gaped open, engulfing Eubuleus's swine before his very eyes; then, with a heavy thud of hooves, a chariot drawn by black horses appeared, and dashed down the chasm. The chariot-driver's face was invisible, but his right arm was tightly clasped around a shrieking girl.

This was the one. The setting was right, the occupations of the witnesses were right. Highly dramatic too. Above all, it encapsulated the enormity and totality of Persephone's disappearance.

As soon as the evening sun neared the horizon and a faint chill came to the air, a young shepherd and his brother who looked after a herd of pigs would leave their father's house and retrace their steps up the hillside, hauling behind them a handcart loaded with extra foodstuffs for their charges. The creatures would gather around their legs and the brothers would count them carefully, checking that all was as it should be. Then, as often as not, the two would sit side by side in the soft grass, chatting together while the beasts munched and, below in the valley, mists would gather and swirl over the winding river.
One night, as the pink in the western sky gave place to encroaching darkness and they rose to leave, suddenly the ground under their feet began

to shudder and a crack appeared in the earth before them. The crack burst wider and became a gaping hole which swallowed up every single one of the herd of swine. They hardly had time even to gasp before their ears were filled with the thunder of galloping hooves, louder and louder. Before their very eyes, a chariot drawn by six black horses appeared over the ridge and dashed into the chasm . . .

And that is more or less precisely how I started. The other experiments were not wasted, for most of them were incorporated into the telling and all had helped to fix key scenes in my head.

Perhaps this view of how I set my starting point has indicated that both the preparation and the telling are more pleasurable than, say, choosing and setting a passage for a comprehension exercise. Certainly the results of storytelling are infinitely more satisfactory in every way. If the pupils simply retell the story, orally *or in writing*, they unconsciously follow the route described above. If I should prefer their versions to the one they have heard from me, then so much the better.

■   THE FOLLOW-UP

It seems appropriate to end with some indication of what followed.

A telling from me can last anything up to forty-five minutes of a seventy-minute lesson. What immediately follows I don't need to plan for: the talk that emerges is usually spontaneous. It may meander on to the end of the lesson, or it may seem right to have the pupils move into groups to talk about some aspect of the story suggested by their first reactions to it. The following lesson is the one which demands more ordered recapping by the pupils, particularly since both in-school and extramural "bunking" is common, not to mention the problem of a flu bug or a dentist's brace or practice for the high-jump on sports day — making it almost certain that some will have missed my telling.

On this occasion I did not ask for a retelling of the story, as I often did, either as I had told it or from a different point of view, or with as many changes as they chose to make (which sometimes produced completely new stories only tenuously connected with the original). But in the course of the recapping I tried to build the whole thing up — from the pupils' own contributions, and from Demeter's viewpoint in particular.

Their first reactions produced a lot of talk about explanations of natural phenomena in different religions, including those practised by the members of that multi-cultural group of children. There was, more specifically, speculation as to whether the ancient Greeks actually believed the Persephone myth. This reflection was brought out in the special moments immediately after I finished telling the story, when the dividing line between reality and fantasy is always blurred. Then they want to say, and occasionally, incredibly, somebody does: "Is that a true story, miss?" And I hardly have time to feel flattered before Lee or Leroy steps in with both feet!

After their initial response, the follow-up veered away in a different direction. I remember sharing various passages and poems with them, one in particular called "Birth Without Violence" by Frederic Leboyer in *Bonds*, The English Project Stage 3 (Ward Lock Educational), which begins with an imaginary conversation about birth:

> "Do you believe that birth is an enjoyable experience . . . for the baby?"
> "Birth? Enjoyable?"
> "You heard me . . . Do you believe that babies feel happy coming into this world?"
> "You're joking!"

It moves on to a kind of medico/speculative monologue about the birth itself.

> This first meeting between mother and child is crucial.
> Many mothers do not know how to touch their babies. Or, to be more exact, do not dare. They are paralysed.
> Many will not admit it, or are not even aware of it. But it is true nevertheless, if you can recognise the signs. Something restrains these mothers, some profound inhibition.
> This new body has emerged from what modesty had led us to call, euphemistically, the "private parts."
> Whatever circumlocution we use, our education has still conditioned most of us to consider these parts of the body as somehow offensive, to reject them; not to mention them.
> That's where the baby has come from.
> From this region of the body that we are supposed to know nothing about, that we don't examine, that we don't display or touch. That we would deny.
> Now this something has emerged from "there." Something warm and sticky. And the result of muscular efforts that resemble those we use in excreting.
> And it is this something we must touch! . . .
> Sometimes one has to take her hands and place them on the child . . .
> The old distinction between good and bad, clean and dirty, permissible and forbidden is dissolved. Suddenly, things are so simple. For the first time in a lifetime.

The last section is an exploration of the mother's first laying of her hands upon her baby. Here are some more extracts:

> The hands that first touch the child reveal everything to it: nervousness or calm, clumsiness or confidence, tenderness or violence.

In attentive and loving hands, a child abandons itself, opens out. In rigid and hostile hands, a child retreats into itself, blocks out the world.

. . . hands that are attentive, alive, alert, responsive to its slightest quiver. Hands that are light. That neither command nor demand. That are simply there. Light . . . and heavy in the weight of tenderness. And of silence.

When the newborn child is placed on her stomach, when she lays her hands on it, she will think: "My problems are over. But not my baby's."
The delivery is over, but the baby's awakening has just begun.

Do not move.
Just be there. Without moving. Without getting impatient. Without expecting anything.

You could have heard a pin drop as I read and they stared at the text. Not much, if any, talk followed. It didn't seem necessary.

I have included these rather lengthy extracts to show what such boys can accept. There were also poems, among them "Little One" by Icilda Eugenie Dunkly in *That Once Was Me*, The English Project Stage 2 book, and "Wedding Wind" by Philip Larkin in *Bonds*. We also revisited a poem which had been chewed over in some detail earlier in the term: "To my Mother" by the West Indian poet E.M. Roach. It is about his dying mother:

It is not long, not many days are left
Of the dead sun, nights of the crumbled moon;
Nor far to go; not all your roads of growth, Love, grief, labour of birth and bone
And the slow slope from the blood's noon
Are shorter than this last.

He tells of her middle years:

I found you strong and tough as guava scrub,
Hoeing the growing, reaping the ripe corn;
Kneading and thumping the thick dough for bread.

He moves on:

I do not mourn, but all my love
Praise life's revival through the eternal year.
I see death broken at each seed's rebirth.
My poems labour from your blood
As all my mind burns on our peasant stock
That cannot be consumed till time is killed.

I saw all this — and so, I hope, did my pupils — as the same texture of stuff that the Demeter myth was made of.

I hope this account has given the flavour of my lessons, though it may have been at the expense of more pragmatic matters like demonstrating the kind of notes I made before telling a story, or describing how I "polished" some bits and left others to chance: to surprise myself in the telling of a tale I was at times careful not to *over*-rehearse in the bathtub or beside the ironing board.

■ PERSONAL RESPONSES

Here are some of the pupils' own words in response to our classroom sharing:

A mother and her kin
huddling together
wondering where the next scrap of grain
is to come from
to feed the mouths of the birds
before they leave the nest
of security.
Each child with nothing,
nothing but their feelings and thoughts.
The mother;
The mother with eyes wholly closed
and head lowered,
bowed down by grief and a tired heart.

Yet she is there,
there for the sharing.
The sharing of thoughts.
The sharing of hunger.
The sharing of love.

John

EBONY

It's nice to have a new born baby sister
enter this ungrateful world.
My mother embraces the baby of youth
and kisses her
on her velvet cheek.
Joy and happiness spread to all the family,
we unite to see the baby.

A small mouth opens to shout out its first cry.
Her rosy wine cheek whines when her first tear

rolls down her small face.
Mum embraces the child
and pats the baby of youth on her back.
I asked mum if I could name my sister.

I named my sister Ebony.
My family liked the name
So we stayed with that name.

Soon, Ebony will grow to be a woman
and the great day will come again
and again and again and again
till our generation dies.

Nicky B

Like a lioness
protecting her cub
threatening to batter any cubs
who decide to play with her cub.
Like a bitch
which cries when a puppy dies
or somebody decides to own it.
Like a cow who milks her calf
and is depressed
when somebody decides
to take it down to the slaughter house.
Like a cat which disciplines her kittens
knowing
they would have to go to another home.

Like a newly born baby
which cries at the smell
of another human being,
a sign that he or she
wants to be with the mother.

Yawi

Here is a mother
An afraid mother
Afraid for her children.
They are starving
She is holding them
like a mother clings to her baby when it is first born.
They are sad.
You can see it in their eyes,
Big eyes
like a mopey dog's
They do not want to be separated

from the one they love so much.
She is the same.
One child is young,
It does not understand.
One child is older,
He understands,
He is mournful.
But
They all have the same feelings.
Sad feelings.

                                    Glen

Six

A STORY READ AND A STORY HEARD

■ TANTALUS

I'm going to tell you about one of the sons of Zeus. And Zeus was the Greek king of the gods. Now Zeus, one way or another, had quite a good life as king of the gods. He did what he liked whenever he liked.

Would you move your chair round a bit? There . . . further back. [giggles] Ready?

And he had lots and lots of sons and daughters, did Zeus, because whenever he took a fancy to some beautiful young woman [giggles], whether it was a mortal woman or a goddess, he thought, right, that's the one for me, at least for the moment, and sure enough there'd be another son or daughter on the scene eventually. To do this he would quite often disguise himself. He disguised himself once — I can't remember exactly what the situation was but I think the father of this girl suspected that there was something likely to happen so he locked her in a room and Zeus got in through some small gap disguised as a shower of gold. On another occasion he disguised himself as a swan. But always he won because he was, after all, the king of the gods and there were many gods and he was very powerful and had a fantastic amount of magic.

Now one of his sons was called Tantalus. Tantalus was of course quite important, being half god, and he was a king; he was king of a place called Sipylus and Sipylus had a huge mountain. Now Tantalus, a bit like his father, liked a good time; he particularly liked wining and dining and entertaining himself with all his friends. He was full of wit — he was himself good company — so Zeus was really quite fond of Tantalus's company: he was one of the sons that Zeus enjoyed being with. So quite often Tantalus would dine on Mount Olympus where the gods lived. He would have quite a lot to do with the gods one way or another. However, at bottom, Tantalus was not the sort of person you and I would like to mix with; he had some very bad streaks in him, and in fact did three things which made Zeus extremely angry and which eventually put Tantalus into a state of eternal torment. I'll tell you what happened.

Tantalus who, as I said, was used to mixing with the gods and dining with them in the great banqueting hall on Mount Olympus, on one occasion was dining with the gods and what a spread! Being gods, they had the most delicate fruits, the most subtle spices from India; being gods, only they would have the richness of these banquets, and above all, the most delightful of all these foods and drinks were ambrosia, the food of the gods — nowhere, but nowhere to be found on earth at all — and nectar, nectar that is found on earth. Nectar is the tiny droplet of sweetness that occurs in flowers; it is that tiny, tiny sweetness which butterflies and insects seek, and bees, when they fumble their way to the very base of the petals. So the gods, being gods, they dined on ambrosia and sweet nectar.

Now on this day at this feast Tantalus thought to himself, "What a lark it would be if my earthly friends could taste the food of the gods." And when no one was looking he stole some ambrosia from the table top and he stole a flask of nectar and he put it in the large pocket of his cloak, and when he left, there it was. But it wasn't exactly when no one was looking, because the gods in a sense are always looking, and the gods knew what he had done; Zeus knew what he had done. But they didn't say anything, not then, anyway.

And the next time that Tantalus had an earthly banquet with his mortal friends, what did they dine on? What did they sup? Ambrosia and nectar! The foods of the very gods! That was the first time that mortal men had supped on such delights.

The next thing that Tantalus did which made Zeus very angry, he stole the golden mastiff that was Zeus's favourite hound, a bright, golden creature — unique — the only one of its kind; pure gold thread was its fur. He stole it away and he hid it and he pretended later on that he'd never even clapped eyes on the golden mastiff. And Zeus was very angry. But he bided his time.

Now the third thing . . .

Are you listening to me, Glen?

The third thing that Tantalus did filled Zeus with fury. It was the third and the last, and for this his father could not forgive him. There came a time when Tantalus invited the gods to eat in his palace in Sipylus. The gods came down, but before they arrived Tantalus had gone to the pantry cupboard to have a look to see what was there and was very upset to discover that there wasn't enough meat for the stew. "What can I do?" thought Tantalus. And then a most evil thought came into his mind. "I could kill Pelops, my son [mutterings: "For the stew!"... giggles], and chop him up and put him in the stew." That, believe it or not, is exactly what Tantalus did: he took his own son and he slit his throat and he chopped him into pieces and he put the pieces into the vast cauldron and made a stew out of his own son! [mounting giggles and muttering: "Every bit, miss!" "Even that." "Give it to the dog." "Kebab!" . . . inaudible comments, giggles]

Now I'll tell you what happened next, because it's quite remarkable. The gods came and they sat at the table and the great cauldron of stew was set in the centre. A bowl of stew was served, was served to each and every one of the gods. But because they were gods they knew, they knew . . . They were very careful with what they ate and they did not eat any portion of Pelops, the young prince, except for one goddess and this was the goddess Demeter who is the goddess of the corn, of the harvest and of the earth's plenty; Demeter was very sad because she had lost her daughter, Persephone, who had gone down to the dark depths of the Underworld to be the wife of the god of the Underworld, Pluto . . . Hades, the king. And she was desperately unhappy. So absorbed was she by her own grief that she didn't notice what the stew was. She took Pelops' left shoulder blade — one of his shoulder bones — and she gnawed it clean. She was the only god who ate any of the meat of Tantalus's son. But what an outrage! What a fearful, fearful thing to do! No one, no one could ever escape from the wrath of the gods for such a deed.

And sure enough, the time came for Tantalus's death. When Tantalus died that was when he received his punishment, for all time. He went past the dog, Cerberus, who sits at the cave mouth, all the way down the dark tunnel to the Underworld, and when he reached the land of the spirits of the dead, there his punishment evolved. There was a great marsh in the Underworld and a huge cliff above the marsh, covered with knotted brambles and nettles. Tantalus was tied, forever, to the branches of a gnarled vine that grew out of the marsh at the base of the cliff. In the marsh there were rivulets of water, which wound their way here and there and some of them were very deep. It was in such a deep gully that Tantalus was tied to the vine.

Sometimes the water washed right up to his very chin and at other times it would recede. And Tantalus suffered forever, forever from excruciating thirst — terrifying, terrible thirst — surrounded by water. Water everywhere. When it came up to his chin he would move his face to try to get his lips to the water but as soon as he got near, as soon as it came up the ridges of his chin, the water would recede and his thirst remained unquenched. Above his head were the branches of the vine winding their way around him and over him and on the vine hung luscious bunches of black, velvety grapes. He would reach up his hand to take a bunch to thrust them against his parched lips, but as he reached his hand up, so the grapes would recede, moving away from his stretched fingers. By that time the water had come back up to his chin. He would think, "I can get it, I can get it! I can drink at last!" But as soon as hands or lips moved towards the water it would trickle away and go down, away into the grey marsh.

For all time he suffered. And for all time, too, beyond the vine on the edge of the cliff, many metres above his head, there stood a great rock, a great rock that had been torn from Mount Sipylus in his own kingdom and brought there to be delicately, dangerously balanced on the edge of the cliff, constantly threatening to fall upon him and crush him down, down to the very depths of the bog. Not just today, not just tomorrow, not just till next week or next month or next year but for all time he suffered this unquenchable thirst with the waters around him and the fruit around him while nothing could touch his lips . . . and up above, a great, menacing dark shape of the huge rock that at any time, so it seemed, might fall on his head.

And that is the end — if end there ever can be — to Tantalus's story but it was not the end of Pelops' story. Pelops lived to become the king of Sipylus in his time because Zeus took pity on the poor young prince who had been chopped into pieces and put in the cauldron. Zeus commanded the gods to put all the pieces back into the cauldron and it was boiled up again — but this time with the magic of Zeus hovering in the air above. Then one god breathed life into the bones and flesh. Demeter, who had been horrified when she learned what she had done, provided an ivory shoulder for Pelops to wear in place of the old one. When all the magic had come to fruition, Pelops rose up out of the cauldron and stood there so fine and youthful and shining that the god Pan played his pipes in joy at the sight. And, as I say, he lived; but it's said that all his offspring were born with an ivory shoulder and so it remained for many, many generations in his family . . . while Tantalus dwelt under the earth, and for all I know, that's where he still is. [*Prolonged silence.*]

> Pupil: Miss, do you believe all that?
>
> Me: Of course!
>
> Pupil: You believe it? [*lots of chortling and mirth*]
>
> Me: Did you believe it?
>
> Pupil: No. [*laughs*]
>
> Me: You're supposed to believe it when you listen, even though you know it's not true.

There. I have turned an oral occasion into a printed story (if you ignore the odd interchange with Glen and company here and there). It is not a piece of high-powered literature, of course. But it is print, and it is narrative — the stuff of English lessons up and down the English-speaking world.

There are important differences between using a printed text and using the spoken word to initiate pupil activity, and I want to examine some of those differences to reveal something of what is lost by what may well be an excessive dependence on printed literature in the classroom.

■ READING VS. HEARING

After typing up this manuscript, I couldn't escape the enormity of the change that had taken place. Though a taped monologue is relatively easy to transcribe, it is still an intensive business. It was not, therefore, until the whole job was done that I was struck — even appalled — by the contrast between the script in my hand and the actuality of the occasion of telling.

There is nothing remarkable about this really: the printed text of any talk wipes out all speech rhythms, tone, pitch, variation of pace, all eye-contact, actions, gestures, mannerisms, physical jerks, quirks, twitches, fleeting grins, frowns, gleams, glares. Indeed, it strikes out completely that entire enigmatic, dynamic container of infinite mysteries — the visible human form. There is a loss of that tangible sense of wonder which Goldsmith expressed over the schoolmaster, though it applies equally well to each and every being, "That one small head could carry all he knew." "Knowing" in the broadest sense.

The most significant moments of the classroom are never recorded in permanent form. It is as though the best things we experience as teachers are like those times when someone says "If only I had a camera!" or "Why on earth didn't we bring the binoculars?" Even the most assiduous and collaborative researcher on the scene is here today and gone tomorrow, unable to touch the totality, the cumulative effect of all the multiplicity of human interactions between the resident participants. And yet it is the best of these interactions that constitute the main reward of being a teacher at all. There is nothing to touch the thrill of having "a good lesson." It is an ephemeral thrill, for when it occurs there is never an approving observer present, no on-the-spot video camera, not even a humble tape recorder conveniently loaded and plugged in, and most certainly no space immediately afterwards in which to attempt to diarize it.

Perhaps that is as it should be. I am reminded of a peripatetic storyteller, Roberto Lagnado, who abandoned English teaching to be paid (initially) pennies for the pleasure of doing what was most satisfying to him. He refused to have any type of recorder near him, ever. He knew full well that if any technological magnifying glass were to inspect his procedure the essence of what he had to bring would petrify. It is the very ephemerality of the storytelling experience that makes it the personal property of the listeners, a special gift, delivered once and left for possessive metamorphosis only within the consciousness of each individual receiver.

And yet, ironically, I find myself about to justify the transcript of the Tantalus story with which I began this chapter. I am glad I have it: it is concrete evidence for me as an English teacher that the spoken, not the written, word is the main source of inspiration to a whole class of children. When it comes to oracy, perhaps it would even be presumptuous to imagine we have very much, if anything, to teach since most people, young and old, are remarkably proficient with oral language. The need is rather to teach ourselves how to set up classroom situations where pupils have plenty to say and where they feel easy about saying it.

But sooner or later we, their teachers, parents, employers, "society," and perhaps most important at this stage, examination boards, expect them to write. Most of our pupils would hardly ever have occasion to write anything significantly communicative if we were not pushing them into it.

The fact is that there are very few pupils who can immediately absorb a written text and feel eager to compose their own as a result, those rare individuals who are able to mull over a text sufficiently to move confidently into writing something for themselves. As English teachers we know that if all our pupils are going to respond to what has been selected for them to read, there must be a period of sharing, of communal mulling over before everyone feels able to write, in pairs, in groups, as a whole class, or even, at times, all three in sequence.

When the storyteller has done, everyone in the class has the capacity to compose. It is my view that the dynamic of listening to a story being told somehow amalgamates the two processes of receiving and reflecting upon the material. Story-hearing cannot be a solitary matter, however; it is essentially and literally communal. There is constant interactive human awareness. Significantly, I found myself irritated by the pace of the taped rendering of Tantalus and the many pauses (it must take less than half the time to read the transcript above than to tell) and yet at the time I felt the pace was right: inside those pauses went the mulling, the mental pictures for each of us. This telling and listening is closer to conversation than to text. The conventional post-stimulus planned group work may be nice, but it is certainly not necessary for the writing task.

Many of the examples of the children's Tantalus work (pages 78-91) will amply illustrate this, as will items elsewhere in these pages. But other features of contrast between the transcript and the classroom telling are worth noting before looking at the final outcome of the lesson. So far I have tried to suggest that a story read, rather than heard, is relatively de-authored and de-humanized. There is a difference between seeing talk and song in letters, on a page, in a book, on a desk, in a classroom, in an institution, and Feste cutting a caper before our eyes in the theatre. More, there is a difference between being informed and personally experiencing. Print is essentially solitary, and if your pupils are like mine they respond to company and immediacy.

Two additional important differences took me very much by surprise when I listened to the tape for the first time. The first has to do with the tone of my voice during most of the story, but particularly at the beginning. The second focuses on my speech rhythms in the high spots, those moments which I hoped in advance would turn out to be my purple passages — for example, the killing and eating of Pelops and above all, of course, the account of Tantalus's punishment.

First, my voice: it sounded as though I was planning a conspiracy with my 4's. I don't mean that I adopted a pose or that here was twee mummy surrounded by her dear little brood listening to a bedtime story (too many streetwise sceptics in the class for that). I think it just happened by instinct. I think the moment you set out to tell a tale, whether it's a personal anecdote from experience delivered in the course of a conversation or a more formal piece of fantasy, you take your listeners into your confidence, trusting them. It's a nice feeling to be on the receiving end. It is warming and calming. It is, dare I add, much different from being the victim (oh dear, surely that's not the right word to use!) of the average classroom procedure. Perhaps this is why even the most restless spirit is likely to be calmed by "Once upon a time . . ." and its more sophisticated equivalents.

I discovered that I had launched this tale in the tone of voice of one in the throes of sharing secrets or juicy bits of gossip. The effect, I suspect, was not only to establish an intimate atmosphere but also to translate the teacher's role to something I have already referred to: the storyteller as the bearer of a personal gift, the more precious for its being short-lived. Such a tone of voice is hardly likely to be used for a written text except as a very obvious and probably uncomfortable affectation.

The second feature — and this really did make me sit up — was that the more I was carried away in relishing the telling, the more rhythmic my voice became. The only clues in the transcript are the obvious (though unplanned) repetitions of some words, apparently for emphasis — which in fact look a bit tawdry in the text. They occur, for instance, in the section about serving up poor Pelops:

A bowl of stew was served, was served to each and every one of the gods.
What a fearful, fearful thing to do!
No one, no one could ever escape from the wrath of the gods for such a deed.

These developed into a kind of elaborate intoning during the description of Tantalus's final plight:

And Tantalus suffered forever, forever from excruciating thirst — terrifying, terrible thirst — surrounded by water. Water everywhere.

And so on. Rhythms, rhythms. All taken very earnestly by 4/R.

As I listened to the tape, my thoughts whooshed right to:

- sitting in Carmel chapel at the age of twelve in Clydach with my Welsh-speaking friends, listening in total incomprehension to the minister's amazing "hwyl";
- the scratched recorded notes of the poet's voice:

I must arise and go now, and go to Innisfree
And a small cabin build there . . .

which my stepson Michael mimics with one hand cupped over his mouth and one finger up his left nostril;

- a sound on Channel Four of an old, grief-stricken Palestinian mother swathed in shawls, wailing the words of her sorrow over the torture of her son by Israeli soldiers;
- Gielgud's refined rendering of blank verse;

■ Alex Pascall's Anansi rejoicing in the sight of a piece of his trickery taking effect:

an' he laaafin', an' he laaafin', an' he laaafin'!

■ a tape we have of the Australian teller and collector of stories, Allan Marshall, and his re-creation of an aboriginal tale-teller of woe and slaughter:

... the Baadoo men they fight and they no go back. The Tootoo men go back. The Baadoo men they kill them in the trees, they kill them on the road. All the way they kill them. They kill them lots. On the beach now. They fight on the beach. They kill them on the beach and over the water they throw their spears. And in the canoes are two Baadoo men. They been married eastern island women and they live in Tootoo and they been left watch canoe. And now the Tootoo men back but only a few back and the few kill the two Baadoo men in canoe and they put their heads make fast with ropes on poles. They stand the poles in the mud and the heads they look at Baadoo. And the bodies they come up and down on the beach and they are no heads. And the Baadoo men they see them lift with the sea and they cry out and they fight in the water. They go in water to chest. To neck. No grip there. They spear up and the Tootoo men in canoes spear down and the Baadoo men kill. And kill. Everyone die. Everyone killed. No Tootoo men live.

And the Tootoo men come - in - and - go - out
Loose - in - the - wa - ter
Dead - in - the - wa - ter
Red - in - the - wa - ter.
All die.

Those last lines are Clydach's Elwyn Jones's hwyl-filled sermonizing, the very same!

Rhythmic speech. Sung, swaying speech. And the baby rocks in her cradle. The disturbed child rocks consolation into himself. The Jewish boy and the Muslim sway and rock into conviction over the open scriptures.

And when I get back to that person called Betty Rosen on the tape, what is so startling to me is to realize that quite inadvertently in my classroom I had become linked to all these others who now peopled my mind, all of them so far removed from me in time, place, motive and talents. Until that listening moment, I think I had thought of rhythm primarily as just another literary device which, along with simile, metaphor, alliteration, metonomy, etc., etc., one learned to define at school. It seems ridiculous that it has taken this long for the impact of its natural function as a release of emotion to dawn upon me. Certainly there is a strong possibility that the encounter with the spontaneous rhythms in storytelling is inextricably

bound up with the natural release of the rhythms of language in my pupils'
own composition, particularly of poetry.

I will conclude with some Allan Marshall observations found on the
tape which contains the Baadoo story:

Nelly said to me once, "Why did you begin this story with an iambic
pentameter?" Well [*he chuckles for a while at this point*] I'm not sure what
that means *yet* — nevertheless, I said [*more chuckling*], "Well, why not?" and
she said it was wrong so I, er, I cut it out . . .

When I was trying to collect stories and I went up into Arnhemland and
moved around with the aborigines, I felt a sudden release because here were
a people that didn't have a written language. Now they spoke with great beauty.
Now people don't realize the wonderful poetry and magic of the way they tell
stories. My father told me once — he used to plait stock whips and he'd plait
'em with kangaroo hide and he used to take the lash and he'd throw the whip
forward and it would descend in a graceful curve and he would say, "See the
fall of that lash? How wonderfully it falls! How beautifully it falls!" One day
he was reading one of my stories and he said to me, "The words fall here
beautifully, Allan." The spoken story, the fall of the words is important, whereas
in the written story the fall of the words is not so important because there is
no sound to show the rhythm and poetry in it. I found that this fall of the words
was very evident in the tales told by the aborigines.

■ A SMALL POINT

When it comes to reading through a printed text in the classroom,
intrusive problems can occur over the meaning of individual words,
problems which need not arise in oral storytelling. Two examples of this
sprang to mind in the telling of the Tantalus story.

There are those words which you know are going to create a diversion.
Typical is the word "gay"; but for the lads in my classes "merry" is archaic
if not actually non-existent. There are countless slang words for the various
bodily functions, which it is as well for the English teacher to keep up with.
A lesson or two after the Tantalus storytelling someone said, "That lump
of rock from that mountain, miss, Syphilis or something, wasn't it, miss?"
Well, that posed no problem — but it could have done during the telling.
Rather than leave Mount Sipylus out, I heard myself change up a gear at
that point just in case, and pronounce the *-us* bit *-oos* as in "puss," just the
way Jason Davies, the Latin teacher, taught us decades ago at Ystalyfera
Grammar.

Then there are the words that provoke that painful pedagogic question:
"Does anyone know what that word means?" It's all very well to tell the
reader who asks the meaning of a word to work it out from the context, but
I suspect that the loss of confidence which comes of failing to understand
words in texts, perhaps frequently, is seriously inhibiting. However, if the

word *recede* pops out in a storytelling, gestures can provide additional context and a few judicious repetitions of the word will ensure that not only will it be understood, it will be found later in the pupils' own work. A told story provides an altogether more effective context for the acquisition of meaning.

Seven

WRITE IT YOUR WAY, NOT MINE

In this chapter I want to illustrate the range in styles of the writing that resulted from my telling of the Tantalus story, not limiting my selection to the most impressive few. As invariably happens after a storytelling, the ability of my pupils leapt out and stared me in the face. I am amazed every time, even though I know it's going to happen. Such things are never recorded in government reports on the low performance of inner-city pupils.

To tell the truth, in spite of the mountain of documentation on the subject, I can't quite believe the "under-achievement" of ethnic minorities. It exists, but I don't think the ethnic minorities are responsible. Ours achieved. Even in terms of the prosaic yardstick of external examinations, standards rose over a five-year period, and by the end of 1985/86, the English Language results in our battered and dying school had lifted themselves well above national average. And why not, pray? Could ideas ever have a richer soil? British though most of my pupils were, they were more yet: Greek Michael Polydorou rubbed shoulders with Turkish Abdullah, with (Afro-)Asian Hitesh, with Twi-speaking Yowi, with Bengali Razwan, with Chinese Wai, with Vietnamese Van Song, with blond, cockney Danny, with Nicky whose granny told him stories whenever he went to visit her in Barbados, with Mauritian Kevin, with Tamil Savarath-erajan (Rajan for short), with St. Vincentian Errol, with Muslim Rashid and Christian Chris, with Jamaican Dennis, Leroy, Sharn, Junior . . . Such variety ensured varied responses and vibrant interchange. Their tales were like them — wide awake and incredibly different one from another.

I had started my term's storytelling at the beginning of September, and when I told the Tantalus story we were all comparatively new to the game.

This is how my lesson notes looked in preparation for that telling on Tuesday, 24 September 1985:

1. Zeus many sons and daughters. Shower of gold. Swan. Favourite son Tantalus king of Sipylus. Good company, wining & dining.
CRIMES of T against Z
   a. ambrosia and nectar
   b. golden mastiff
   c. Pelops chopped up for stew. Demeter ate.
T's PUNISHMENT — marsh, deep creeks, grapes. Rock above.
Pelops rose again to become king of Sipylus.

2. Discuss best bits??

3. Write in pairs, a good bit; poetry???

The group's first application to written work was 3 above. I shall focus for a moment on what they did, partly to illustrate the vividness of the immediate mental pictures which arose from hearing the story, and partly as a reminder of the "mixed-ability" nature of the group. These are complete quotations, warts and all, from the bits of scrap paper they wrote on, representing the most able, the most sinful, a lazybones, and the one who most desperately feared putting pen to paper:

The sweetness of this godly juice
was not for mortal lips.
Pale translucent yellow
is lapping
gently
in the golden goblets.

Gary and Kin Tai

Tantalus hung there dying of thirst and hunger. A grape vine hung above him. He was trying to reach out for the grapes but they moved up away from him. The water around him rised up to his chin as he bent over to drink it, it went away. As he was gazing away he saw a great big rock balancing on the edge of the cliff hanging over the edge ready to crush him any minute. Tantalus was sweating, sweat was running down his forehead.

Robert and Evren

There he was, Pelops
Rising made of steam.
All the gods smiled.
Some laugh'ed with joy

As they cast more spells
He became real once more.

Then they noticed he had only one shoulder.
A godess gave him a shoulder of ivory
So all his offspring had ivory shoulder's
And they lived and danced once more.

Stuart and Ercan

Tantalus Decibed to Hold a Banquet for some Gods But his di'nt have enough meat for his stew. So he thought that he would CuT up his son pelops. He was sleeping alone when his father cript up on him. Tantalus was carrying a buttchers knife as sharp as a razor.

Tantalus slowly brought the knife across his throat and pelops his son lay dead.

Tantalus dragged his son across the flor to the kitchen.

(This last sample was written by a pupil with a support teacher who provided the correct spelling of words only when requested — normally he would have managed only a few words in the time!)

This writing was done during the last few minutes of the same lesson in which I told the story. It was in the following lesson that the pupils got down to the real business of retelling. After some brief recapping I asked them to grip their pens, their rough paper, any notes from working in pairs during the previous lesson, and retell the story of Tantalus, if possible from the point of view of one of the participants rather than just as narrator. And off they went.

That was the sum total of preparatory work for this task outside my actual storytelling, except for one more bit. During the second part of that first lesson we had chatted about moments in the story which different boys claimed to have visualized most clearly. These, predictably, turned out to be the killing of Pelops, Demeter chomping at the shoulder bone, and Tantalus's final punishment. Quite a few were intrigued by the golden mastiff, so I added a little more detail which I had accidentally omitted — no doubt out of indecent haste to get on to the high drama! Needless to say, I also provided them with the word *tantalize*, which several writers picked up to use later, noticeably Glen (see below) who did so gleefully, almost as an Aesopian moral to his story.

They got down to the job of writing very readily, with none of the signs of reluctance or doubt: not a single "But I don't know what to write, miss." They knew all right. Most of them took their stories home to finish and they reached me some days later.

Michael Polidorou brought his to my office just before the official start of school on the following Friday morning. It is not the polished artifact of a high flyer but just Michael pouring it all out in a continuous flood (the paragraphing is mine); he has a lot to learn. It is highlighted here because it typifies in a patchwork the literary potential of the kind of north London lad I have come to know so well.

■ MICHAEL P'S STORY

Many, many years ago in Greece the gods in the heavens would dine and sing together and dance to Greek music. The god Zeus who was god of all the gods lived in the heavens. He was one of the most handsome of the gods. He had many lovers and many sons and daughters; he always found a way of meeting these beautiful girls. Fathers had tried to stop the god Zeus from loving their daughters. Sometimes Zeus would change his shape to something nice like a swan. One man locked his daughter in a room to stop him but Zeus changed to a steam and flew through the cracks, through the walls, and then he loved her.

Zeus also had a few friends, like a king called Tantalus. He owned a small city behind a mountain called Sipylus. It was large if you were not in it but it was small compared to other cities. Sometimes Zeus was kind to Tantalus and allowed Tantalus to visit him and they would eat ambrosia and drink nectar and talk about their women. One day he visited Zeus and Zeus asked him if he would look after his golden mastiff. Tantalus agreed and two weeks later he was supposed to bring it back. Weeks went by. Zeus was sad but not angry. "I will go and visit Tantalus," said Zeus. When he arrived he asked him, "Where is my golden mastiff? You were supposed to bring him back days ago."

"What golden mastiff? I don't know no golden mastiff. I don't even know what it is," said Tantalus.

Zeus disappeared. He appeared again on Mount Olympus. He was not pleased. Two days later Tantalus was invited again to Mount Olympus to a dance. He went and, when all the guests were gone, Tantalus stole the nectar drink and some ambrosia and made a run for it. Even this didn't anger Zeus. He was interested in the way Tantalus lived and so he was invited to a party at his palace.

Meanwhile Tantalus was making a meal of chops with pitta bread then he realized that he had run out of meat. He had just started so he thought of finding meat but the shops were all closed and the meat market was closed because it was Sunday so he thought again. Later he looked at his son Pelops sitting on the grass. Pelops was young and a lazy boy — not even the maids were that lazy.

And then the most dreadful idea ever came into his mind. You see, I know this because I am Zeus and I know what he was thinking. I saw. He crept behind him and cut his throat. Later he sliced the meat off Pelops to pieces and cooked them. I then told the other gods and goddesses not to eat the meat. When we got there Tantalus seemed quiet and he hardly spoke. Then he called out. "Come, let us eat!" he shouted.

"Yes!" shouted the goddess Demeter. I remembered that Demeter was away when we watched Tantalus chop his son to pieces.

We sat at the table and began eating. We ate the pitta bread and the turkey he had cooked. None of us except Demeter was eating the meat. I tried to tell her not to eat it but it was too late: Demeter had gnawed the flesh to the bone. Then Tantalus stood up and said, "Come, my friends, eat the beautiful meat. People of this kingdom have hunted for it for days and they would give anything for it."

I grew mad with anger. Not only does he kill his son but he lies about it, too. I stood in fury. Lightning struck the table and Tantalus was shaking. "I, Zeus, sentence you to judgement!" With the sky roaring, Tantalus fell to his knees and begged for mercy. He vanished.

Then he appeared before me. The room was dark and cold. It was raining and lightning was the only light. I looked at him and said, "Tantalus, you were once my friend but you have made a lot of mistakes. Tantalus, you stole my dog and denied it. You stole my food and denied it. You killed your son in cold blood and lied that it was hunted."

The gods said, "Guilty!" and he was gone.

Now he lives in a dark cave tied to a wall of bricks with chains. Above him lies a grape tree with large juicy grapes and beneath him a river cool in water. Darkness surrounds him. No food, no drink, no rest till the thousands and thousands of years he has to serve have passed. The grapes will fall down and split and as he reaches the chains stretch out further then stop a few inches from his feet and the river goes higher to his neck and then to his knees and he cries while above his head a huge mountain is sitting on the edge of this crater, falling, then lifting back again. This is his torture.

Pelops was remade with an ivory shoulder given by Demeter and his family will always have one.

Now Tantalus is 5001 years old and has been removed from his torture. He was sent to a small room and was magically clothed in black robes. "Tantalus, you killed your son and now you must be chained to these new walls top and bottom until I find a new torture," I said.

"I hate you, Zeus! I hate you!" shouted Tantalus.

From that day he was in a tiny room with two men called Bid and Bod. They chained him to a wall with chairs across his stomach. On the sides of these chairs were chains pulling him first at one side then to the other. When he was on the right the chains pulled him to the left.

The next day Demeter was speaking to my wife who had made a new palace two mountains away and she wanted a tunnel through the mountain. Then an idea struck me — why not put Tantalus and the other criminals to work? Demeter agreed. I summoned Delon who was the master of punishments. Now Tantalus was with three criminals. Work had started and I put a whip into the hand of Delon and he cracked this on the back of Tantalus. Together the three worked for days making the tunnels through the mountains. Inside the mountains were devils who tormented them by rebuilding the rock wall. They would scream and this was another danger. Horace, the thief, collapsed, and I dismantled the chains to free him before he died of his laziness. Then we placed him in a tomb because he always wanted to die in a tomb.

One day the tunnel was finished. Tantalus pressed himself against the wall and the large cave collapsed on top of him and killed him instantly. Now he is in hell, burning to the end of time.

My advice to you mortals of the twentieth century is — don't trust Greek builders. THE END

When we passed each other in the corridor, immediately after I had finished my first lesson of the day, out rang the familiar cri de coeur, "Have you read it yet, miss? Did you like it, miss?"

"I've been teaching since I last saw you, haven't I? Honest to god, I'll read it by our next lesson and that's a fact." I was visualizing Michael's pages of continuous scrawl, which tended to make me place his book on the bottom of the pile.

"Cheers, miss!" and he scuttled off.

Still, it proved to be an intriguing read, as I hope you agree. I will not labour my way through a critique, but certain features deserve comment, features which I have often observed in the work of these young people and which enable them to produce polished prose and poetry of real quality as they become more mature writers.

There are poetic rhythms in the opening lines. Michael is able to adopt this flow appropriately when he feels like it:

"Tantalus, you stole my dog and denied it. You stole my food and denied it. You killed your son in cold blood and lied that it was hunted."

Darkness surrounds him. No food, no drink, no rest till the thousands and thousands of years he has to serve have passed.

And there are several more. There are moments when he sounds truly poetic — I'm not sure whether it is by design or, if such is even possible, by accident:

. . . beneath him a river cool in water.

Zeus changed to a steam and flew through the cracks, through the walls, and then he loved her.

Is the latter all that far, in vision if not precisely in language, from these lines by Tennyson which leapt into my mind when I read that sentence by Michael?

A land of streams! some, like a downward smoke,
Slow-dropping veils of thinnest lawn, did go

The Lotus-Eaters

Some significant aspects of the story he completely ignores, or perhaps misses altogether: that Tantalus was the son of Zeus and that Demeter was too grief-stricken over the loss of Persephone to abstain from the Pelops meat. Michael explains the whole thing a new way. Other facts of the story he digests and interprets in the light of everyday experience:

... and they would eat ambrosia and drink nectar and talk about their women.

... when all the guests were gone, Tantalus stole the nectar drink and some ambrosia and made a run for it.

... but the shops were all closed and the meat market was closed because it was Sunday.

Then quick as a flash his mobile mind incorporates lazy maids: I doubt whether Tottenham could boast of a maid, lazy or otherwise, in any household! What I find particularly attractive is that this boy of Greek parentage was the only one to emphasize the Greekness of the story; he has his Tantalus busy with pitta bread — just like home. And when it comes to his "funny" portion, carefully announced by the appearance of Bid and Bod, it is the concluding sentence which comes off — though if the same thing had been written by anyone else, not least by one of my Turkish-Cypriots, there would have been trouble in the camp!

There was a good deal of humour amongst these boys and also a wonderful willingness to draw upon real experience when writing in English lessons, the latter an indispensable feature of their contributions in coursework folders submitted as part of the competitive external examination scene. On those occasions when I have been the English Language external examiner to far posher schools than ours, allotting justifiably high grades to very competent, literary submissions which have bored me cross-eyed, I have returned to my everyday piles of marking with relief.

As a final, minuscule feature, I must add that these kids were nothing if not crafty. Michael was so busy enjoying himself (another skill possessed in abundance by these fellows) he quite forgot that he was supposed to write as a participant rather than a narrator, so he worked in his change of identity with "You see, I know this because I am Zeus" just before the covert slaughter of Pelops.

What is so interesting to me in all this is that, where others established and maintained a particular style or mode throughout (see Chris's elegy, John's dignity of language, Earl's colloquial approach, Roger's poetry, etc.), Michael's piece has elements of this whole range. He has, therefore, the means at his disposal to concentrate on any one style should he decide to do so, or should such demands be made of him.

■ OTHER STORIES

Some of the boys, like Michael, beavered away for page after page. Some limited themselves to a very specific and less narrative route. Here is a short but effective lament by a father for his prodigal son. It is hard to realize that this resulted from precisely the same stimulus as Michael's did:

Oh, how my heart grieves for my son Tantalus for he has sinned. He took the ambrosia off of my table, the finest ambrosia you could find. He took it for his own purpose. But I, I will leave this for another time.

Alas, alas my son Tantalus has taken the dog, the only dog with gold hair that glitters; but he denies that he has it. I asked him to look after the dog but he now keeps it for himself.

Dear, oh dear, how so much sorrow has come to me from my son. He has now gone to the extreme. He has taken my grandson, Pelops, and slaughtered him just to use him in his stew. How evil of him! I shall not let this pass without punishment. After his great banquet I shall give him the punishment he deserves. It hurts me even to think of what will occur to him. This has brung shame upon the family.

That is enough of Tantalus, my son.

Chris

I learned quite early on that Chris's family are very devout Christians; it is possible that the tone of this, as set (and sustained throughout) in the very first sentence, owes as much to his reading of the Bible as it does to hearing a pagan story. What I particularly like is the sensitivity he shows to a parental viewpoint: I can certainly respond, as a mum, to the start of the third paragraph and — a much more subtle matter — to the sorrowing that comes on perceiving one's child suffer on account of his or her own shortcomings and blunders. Every mother's son may not commit ugly murder, but one's children do have a tendency to horrify one from time to time!

In Mustafa's version the boot is on the other foot:

How could he do this to me? Me, his only son, his one and only son! Banishing me to the underworld! I don't deserve this. While I am waiting to die in this godforsaken place I may as well tell you why I'm here.

It all started when my father, Zeus, invited me to dinner. Of course, I immediately accepted his invitation.

"Ah, my son, come in and sit down."

"Thank you, father."

"Have some nectar to wet your throat, my son."

"Mmmmm!" This stuff's lovely. I'll take some later.

"Have some ambrosia."

"Thank you."

"Mmmmm! Mmmmmm!" This stuff's beautiful — I'll nick some of this later, as well.

"Well, I'm just going to the toilet, if you'll excuse me, my son?"

"Of course. Go ahead."

"Phew, he's gone, I'd better move fast. Oh, I've spilt some — better get it cleaned up quick!"

"Er . . . I'll have to be off, father. Thanks for everything." Including the ambrosia and nectar.

That was my first offence. My second was when my father asked me a favour.

"Could you look after my golden dog, my son?"

"Of course, my pleasure." My pleasure indeed, what a beautiful golden hound! He's not getting this back.

While Mustafa's Tantalus gloats in his greed, Yowi's is rather more reflective:

My life was not the best of lives. As some people would say I was born with a silver spoon. I was born to a very powerful god, Deuce. Deuce was a very kind father. I got everything I wanted. I never starved. I always had the best. I was actually spoilt rotten: I did not respect my parents or any of the other gods.

Eventually I grew up into a fine young man. I had the best gold, everything, but I still wanted more. One day when my dad left Greece to go to Egypt he asked me to look after his golden dog which was very beautiful. I agreed to look after it so my dad sent the dog to me with one of his servants.

When he came back from Egypt he sent a servant to collect the dog but I denied that I had ever laid my eyes on that golden dog. My dad, being a very kind god, forgived and forgot.

One day I was asked to wine and dine with the gods. At the dinner there was Ambrosia, the food of the gods, which did not exist on earth; it was only for the mouth of a god. And there was nectar, the sweetness in a flower when you put it in between the gaps of your teeth and suck. No ordinary mortal had ever tasted these foods.

Glen's style is much more snappy and succinct:

The third thing I did was the worst. You see, I was holding a feast and had invited all my father's godly friends (and my father, of course) but when I looked I had no meat to make the stew. So as there was no meat around the palace I did a very stupid thing. I cut my son Pelops' throat, chopped him into small pieces, boiled him and stewed him. My father found out! This was too much, so, when I died I came down to this place where I suffer eternally from torment. I can reach water and food but every time I go to cup my hands or draw near to it they pull back. So, never do stupid things like I have done or you will suffer a similar torment and will be TANTALIZED!

Roger, on the other hand, lets language roll around him:

I said to him, "You are banished from this country and the penalty is death!"
He was brought up to the top of Mount Olympia and there was a hole full
of darkness and fumes of anxiety, the bloodthirsty breath of the hole. In the
hole was stairs leading right down to the underworld. The place of death. He
walked down the stairs and that is all I saw of his life . . .

He was at the bottom of the underworld.
Darkness turned in horror
The vines holding him tight
The air saturated of evil.

Still there it was
Right above, in the corner of his eye
A heavy boulder of rock, full of evil.
His eyes steamed with despair.

The great marshy waters
Breathing out hatred,
The darkness of the spirits
Forever surrounding him.

Kevin Soobadoo will always lap up a good tale and sees it in his head,
image after image:

Tantalus, Tantalus, my cruel son Tantalus! I never want to see him again
in the land of the gods! I shall never forgive him for what he has done. His
cruelty makes my blood boil — it's like my own blood being cruel.
I shall never forget when Tantalus, my own son, committed his first offence
or shall I put it, his first cruelty offence. I remember all the gods were sitting
round the large, bulky, varnished wooden table eating our favourite dish, sweet
thick nectar and indescribable ambrosie. These two as a combination were
absolutely delicious. Tantalus was not a god so he wasn't allowed to eat these
foods but when he heard about them his mouth would water. One day Tantalus
sat down and thought to himself, if I was to take some of this delicious food
down to earth ordinary people will be able to taste some of this food of the
gods. Well, it's not as if the gods would be missing anything, they have jars of
the stuff.
So one day Tantalus crept into the kitchen and on the table he saw two
huge jars of ambrosia and nectar. No one was looking so he quickly and sharply
dashed them into his velvet black cloak. He then rushed down Mount Olympus,
thinking no one had seen him but I, burning in fury, had seen every step and
thought which he had taken.
A few months later I kept on noticing that Tantalus was looking a bit
miserable. This went on for about one month then I suddenly had an idea for
stopping the depression. I'd lend him my great golden dog who cheers up everyone. So the next day I told Joshua, my private servant, to lend Tantalus the
golden dog . . .

Next come some very different images from Gary, the class bookworm. This is how he began his retelling:

Sometime after the banishment of Tantalus there was a feast. All the splendour fit for the gods was laid down on the banqueting table. There was roast ox, pork done so that it was a crisp brown and it smelt delicious, succulent beef flavoured with spices from all over the country. There were delicacies such as chilled crab, boiled prawns, all to be washed down with the sweetest, reddest of red wine. All this for the birth of Pelops' son, Hannibal.

Now Hannibal was the spitting image of his great grandfather, Zeus, who had personally blessed him. He had pure blue eyes and short dark hair, smooth creamed skin. As Hannibal grew up, Zeus would visit him and spend hours in his company, watching him duel with his closest friend Jason, the son of Sheila, lady in waiting to Pelops' wife . . .

On one such visit Zeus caught Hannibal alone with his thoughts. "Ah ahum!" Zeus gestured to him.

"Sorry, sire, I was miles away."

After a pause, Hannibal looked at Zeus and spoke. "Sire, what happened to Tantalus, my grandfather?"

The smile which had been on Zeus's face vanished. His face became a mask of seriousness . . .

John, too, is never short of originality or the words to express it. He chose to tell the story through Athena:

"Athena," said Zeus. "Where is your brother, Tantalus?"

"I will fetch him, father."

"Tantalus, we shall dine tonight. Eat to your heart's content. We shall kill the ambrosia and sip the nectar of life, life and body. We shall eat the food of the gods."

"No, father. You must come and eat with me in the palace of Sipylus and we shall feed on stew. My food is not as yours, Zeus, but your presence in my home is a true honour. Bring the gods to my house."

"I shall look forward to that."

"So shall I, Athena."

The gods arrived at the house of Tantalus and in the centre of the circular table there stood a cooking pot. I saw Apollo look at Zeus in dismay and Zeus just said, "I know."

I took the first helping from the stew, making sure I chose carefully as I knew the ingredients. The tender meat which was placed in front of us was Pelops, son of Tantalus.

"Salty," came a sharp remark from Demeter, "the meat is salty." Demeter's mind was on other things . . . Glances fired across the table and throughout the meal. Not a word was said except when Zeus was ordering wine. Demeter unknowingly had gnawed the shoulder bone of Pelops now.

Tantalus was called out of the room by a servant. There, at the palace gates, was a peasant clutching a golden dog. "Here is the wretched beast, now give me the nectar and ambrosia."

"You have done well to bring me the mastiff. I am sure the food will be rewarding."

As this was going on Zeus and I were watching and listening through the magic created by Apollo. When Tantalus came back into the room Neptune, who was sitting patiently through all these goings on, made lightning with his hands and threw it at Tantalus's heart. Zeus caught the bolt of lightning before it hit Tantalus and destroyed it.

"Why did you stop me from killing him, Zeus? Why?"

"Do not question me, Neptune," said Zeus. "I will decide his punishment. Death is far too good for him. I have something else in mind."

Zeus rubbed his hands into a ball and opened them slowly. A picture formed between his two hands. The picture was of Tantalus. He was tied up to a tree with a stream running along at his feet.

From distant Ancient Greece to more familiar matters of today — or at least Earl's chatty style would make it seem so:

"Grandad, what is this drink? It tastes of paradise."

"It's nectar, my lad, nectar."

"Where does it come from? I've never heard of such a thing."

"It comes from the precious flowers in my garden of gods. You like it?"

"It's beautiful. May I take some back to the ground with me so my friends can have some?"

"No. This is a big secret. You must not even tell your father about it. This must be between me and you and all the other gods."

"Okay. Can I have a little bit more, then?"

"Here you are, then you'd better go. It's getting late."

"Okay. Bye, Goldie."

"Wuff! Wuff!"

"Goodbye, grandad. See you tomorrow."

I took the stairs to earth and ran back home. "Dad! Dad, I had a good time at grandad's. I had a taste of one of his finest drinks of wine. I tasted this wine made out of — ooops! I'm not allowed to tell you — but it was out of this world — ooo, well."

"What is this drink, my boy?"

"I'm not allowed to tell you!"

"Guards, strip him to his pants! Now. What is this drink? Tell me, boy, tell me."

It would be true to say that many wrote clear, easy-flowing accounts, quite close to the "original," but coming into their own at the climax of the drama. Tony's, which fits that pattern, will make a fitting conclusion to this series of extracts from the work of my pupil authors:

When I arrived with the rest of the gods Tantalus welcomed us into his house and we sat down to eat his food. All of us knew what Tantalus had done so we didn't eat the meat except for Demeter. She was so full of grief because she had lost her daughter to the king of the underworld that she didn't think of what she was eating. She ate the whole of Pelops' right shoulder. After we had finished our meal I started an argument with Tantalus. I got so angry that I banished him to the underworld.

On the way down Tantalus could see this long winding path that he just floated along. When he got to the mouth of the kingdom of the underworld he stopped moving and there was a ferocious dog. Suddenly a tree started to wrap itself around Tantalus. After he had been tangled up the level of the water there started to rise until it reached his chin and hundreds of bunches of luscious grapes grew above his head. Everytime he tried to get a drink the water receded and everytime he reached for some grapes the branches of the trees would recede. There was also a giant rock dangling above his head. It was a piece of the mountain Sipylus where his castle was.

Tantalus is still down there being tortured of thirst, hunger and fear.

These are but samples of an enormous variety of approach and therefore of language. While in Michael Polidorou's retelling there are variations in style as his whim shifts, each of the other examples here is from a story which maintains its stance and tone virtually throughout.

And what a range there is! Perhaps the stateliest is John's, which he chose to fix firmly in a classical setting — though I suspect that it was by accident rather than design that his compression of the ambrosia/nectar and golden dog affairs into five cryptic lines ensured a preservation of the unities! There are none of the elisions of speech in his dialogues, his sentence structures are often complex and everywhere controlled, and his language throughout maintains a fitting dignity. Others who are clearly aiming for a serious tone do not always sustain it: Gary's "Hannibal was the spitting image of . . ."; Kevin S's ". . . they have jars of the stuff"; Yowi's "I was actually spoilt rotten."

But having noted these little stumbles, I would not want to detract from what the writers have achieved:

Yowi creates a sombre mood in presenting his over-indulged child: "I did not respect my parents or any of the other gods . . . I denied that I had ever laid my eyes on that golden dog . . . My dad, being a very kind god, forgived and forgot . . ." are solemn words, and his repeated references to Zeus's kindness underline the ingratitude of the son's behaviour.

In addition to the elevated language of his narration (". . . banishment . . . feast . . . splendour fit for the gods . . . laid down on the banqueting table . . . Zeus, who had personally blessed him . . . sire . . . His face became a mask of seriousness . . ."), Gary lends weight to his account by structural tricks such as placing a short, significant statement ("All this for the birth of Pelops's son, Hannibal") after a piece of sensuous description.

Kevin, whose sense of fun is never very far off whatever he writes, yet has the capacity to be both succinct and portentous when necessary: ". . . but I, burning in fury, had seen every step and thought which he had taken." His opening paragraph has something of the remarkable declamatory quality maintained throughout Chris's Greek chorus-like interpretation of the tale, after which he makes a shift, quite successfully I think, to a more confiding narrative style.

On the face of it, *Mustafa's* style is chatty in the extreme, compared, say, with *John's*: "I may as well tell you . . ." speaks directly to the reader, who is allowed into his thinking ("Including the ambrosia and nectar" and "My pleasure indeed"); yet many of his expressions lend ironical drawing-room manners to his presentation, while there is no letup in courtesy between father and son, whether it's a visit to the lavatory or a piece of pilfering that's on the cards.

All these are very far removed from the everyday conversation occurring in *Earl's* retelling, which even includes a "Wuff! Wuff!" from the dog, and an "ooops," followed by the ignominious baring of a bottom! This is the way Earl thinks of stories, essentially close to real life come what may: retelling makes room for all levels of sophistication.

Further removed again is *Roger's* eager grasp of the chance to use richly emotive language: ". . . a hole full of darkness and fumes of anxiety . . . bloodthirsty breath . . . Darkness turned in horror . . . The air saturated of evil . . . His eyes steamed with despair . . ." I must admit that coming across this kind of writing in a pile of everyday marking gives me a real thrill, and I believe then I am lucky to be in a position to encounter such creativity.

In addition to these stylistic features, it is interesting to consider how far the pupils have altered events in the story they heard in the classroom. The changes are many, even among the very few samples of work I have included. Most changes don't amount to major alterations, but to the presentation of what I would call "revisioning" by individual pupils. Yet many of them come close to changing the facts. *Tony*, an unusually conscientious and dutiful pupil, would have made it his business to stick to my "correct" version and yet he makes some noticeable shifts:

Me: He went past the dog, Cerberus, who sits at the cave mouth . . .

Tony: [*Having already gone down the path*] When he got down to the mouth of the kingdom of the underworld he stopped moving and there was a ferocious dog.

Me: He went all the way down the dark tunnel to the Underworld . . .

Tony: On the way down Tantalus could see this long winding path that he just floated along.

Me: Tantalus was tied, forever, to the branches of a gnarled vine that grew out
of the marsh at the base of the cliff.

Tony: Suddenly a tree started to wrap itself around Tantalus.

(I prefer his version — which often happens!)

These are actually very slight changes. Michael makes many changes,
notably a major addition to the events at the end of the story. Roger sends
Tantalus down a volcano-like hole in Olympus. Kevin S has Zeus lending
the golden mastiff in order to cure Tantalus's depression. John makes so
many changes, even in the short extract from his story, that they hardly
warrant listing here. Gary provides a totally invented opening, with a new
situation and new characters from a later period in time. Most interesting,
I think, is Earl's retelling: though it is not in him to rise to the heights of
fantasy, his more earthbound imagination has also made an original and
entertaining opening which has Zeus sharing the secret of ambrosia and
nectar not with Tantalus but with Pelops, which in turn becomes a source
of contention in the Sipylus household and, of course, goes on to produce
even more divergence from the story as told by me. This is inventiveness
indeed.

I have spent time here pointing out the range of this writing, both in
style and in imaginative leaps away from the received story. My experience
tells me that a told story gives rise to a wider scope of responses than any
other language stimuli in the repertoire of an English teacher.

Two more observations. First, there is a marked difference between
these pieces and what emerged when the boys were two years younger.
Remember the 1/U's whose writing of "Abit's story" produced a fairly
consistent style across the board — homely, human tales by real villagers;
this remained true even when a story I told them was much further from
reality than Abit's story. And though the pupils had complete freedom in
retelling it, there was only one example of a significant change in the
basics of the story — Dennis' incorporation of the benign wandering
stranger whose presence allowed a happy ending. The difference says quite
a lot about the pupils' linguistic and intellectual development over a two-
year period, a development which is not always given enough scope in more
conventional classroom activities than story retelling.

Second, the capacity to produce sophisticated varieties of style and
originality — so much demanded in the coursework requirements of
examination boards — can easily become a range *within each individual's
performance over a period of time* (see the potential in Michael's story)
because models have been produced by the pupils themselves and not
superimposed from the outside. Instead of being intimidated by the quality
or unfamiliarity of an unknown author's creation, pupils say to themselves,
"If Chris (or Roger) can write like that, so can I." Quite simply, the teacher

can exploit a particularly distinctive retelling from a pupil by making it the focus of a whole lesson in preparation for the next writing task.

So what exactly is here? I ask myself. Intimations of immortality? Well, sometimes when I'm reading through a set of folders or exercise books I think so! Why not over-estimate pupils' possibilities? It's better than being saddled with low expectations.

Eight

CHOOSING A "GOOD" STORY

One of the criteria for choosing stories to tell, as I have said, is one's own enjoyment. Even the title of "The Land Where No One Ever Dies" has a resonance reaching into that most awesome bit of our inside which never quite grasps the horrible mystery of our own mortality. It is the leading bait of the Mormon on your doorstep. As for the tale itself, suffice it to say that when I first heard it, read by John Berger during a TV documentary, my teacherly soul shouted "Eureka!" This was gold — as far as I was concerned at any rate. I would not be needing the receptive soil of a 1/U for such stuff to take instant hold. Hearing it was followed by a frantic search for the memo pad and pen which only in theory live next to the phone and by a frenzied scribbling, scribbling to get the "facts" down intact. I would tell it to the first class to come under my nose next morning and throw all other lesson plans to the winds. This was exactly and precisely my kind of story. It was irresistible.

What makes a "good story" good is hard to pinpoint. There is a wealth of "lit crit" (and plenty of students of rhetoric — or linguistics or narratology) which never quite gets to the heart of it. Teachers and storytellers will fail, however, if they don't choose their subject matter with the aid of some trustworthy criteria. I can only guess at what magnetized me first to the particular tale of this chapter *and* delighted every listener I've ever had in front of me, whether ten-year-old, teenager or adult, with or without English as the first language. But before I examine my guesswork, let me give you the story.

THE LAND WHERE NO ONE EVER DIES

In a village long, long ago — in northern Italy, I think it was — there lived a boy who knew everyone thereabouts and they all knew him. All the faces of the people were familiar. That's how it is in little villages, not at all like in cities. The seasons came and went. When the heavy rains fell, the little stream that ran through the village scurried at a great rate, but when the sun beat down only a trickle was left to meander about among the hot, bald stones of the stream's bed. A stranger visiting the village from time to time would find everything pretty much the same from year to year. But things did not remain the same — nothing ever does. New life came into the world, people grew older — even wiser sometimes — and old folk shrank and died. That's just what happened one autumn evening to the boy's grandmother. Her death made the whole family mourn because they loved her very much, and she was especially precious to her favourite grandson.

The boy became very thoughtful. He decided that he wanted to stay in the world for longer than his grandmother had. He wanted to stay forever. "It seems," he thought, "from what people say and even from what I see for myself that hereabouts death comes to everyone sooner or later." So he asked his parents what he could do about this. "There must be somewhere where I could live forever."

"Oh no," said his mother and father, "there is nowhere. One day you must die like everyone else."

But this was no answer for the boy. He said, "I am going to try. There must be somewhere. There must be a land where no one ever dies and I am going to find it for myself."

He said goodbye to his mother and father, to his brothers and sisters, and he left all the neighbours, all his friends and relations to begin his long search. No one could help him, no one, until one day he came across an old man with a beard resting on his chest and this old man was pushing a wheelbarrow full of boulders and rubble. The boy greeted the old man and told him of his search.

"I am looking for a land where no one ever dies. I do not want to die."

The old man said, "You could stay with me if you wish. You see that mountain?" He pointed towards a hillside nearby where there were many rocks and stones crumbling and tumbling down a steep slope. "I am moving the whole of it, spreading it over the plain and one day that mountain will be level. You can stay and help me move its stones away and away. That will take a long time — and only then will you die."

"How long will it take?" asked the boy.

"About a hundred years I would say."

"That won't do for me," replied the boy, and he took his leave of the old man and continued his journey.

In the distance he could see a vast forest. Soon he found himself swallowed up by its trees. There he came across an old man with a beard down to his middle and a large pruning knife in his right hand. "Good day to you, sir," said the boy, but the old man hardly looked up from his work, which seemed to be to prune back all the branches from a tree. "I wonder if you could help me," continued the boy. "I am trying to find a place where I can live forever."

"Then stay with me," replied the man. "You will die only when I have cleared away this whole forest."

"How long will that take?" asked the boy.

"Two hundred years or so, and I reckon no one but a madman would want to live longer than that."

"It's not long enough for me," said the boy, and he went on his way.

After much travelling he reached a wide sea which disappeared over the edge of the distant horizon. He stood where the little grey waves lapped against the gravelly shore and gazed across the expanse of ocean. As he turned to walk on, he saw ahead of him the oldest man he had ever met in his life with a beard that came down to his very knees. The man's eyes were fixed upon a duck which, at his feet, was drinking from the little waves that trickled over the coarse sand, lapping up the water of the ocean into his flat beak. The boy asked his question yet again. "Can you help me, sir? I am looking for the land where I will never die."

"This spot is surely good enough for you. I am waiting for the day when this little duck has drunk the whole ocean dry. Stay with me and only then will you die."

"How long will that take?" asked the boy.

"I would guess three hundred years. At the end of such a time you will be tired enough of life and ready to move on."

"No, no," replied the boy, "I must go on with my search. I do not want to die at all, not ever." And with that he left.

Farther off from the great ocean he could see a high mountain. As he came nearer he saw there was a castle on the top of it and a little track that wound its way up to its entrance. He stared at the twisting road and at the castle swathed in shifting clouds and he had a feeling in his bones that his journey was soon to end.

His pace quickened and soon he was climbing up the ragged path, over the stones and potholes. It was a long, slow haul up that winding way and beside the road were muddy ditches. Eventually he reached the oaken door of the castle and banged upon it as loudly as he could with his small fist. He heard footsteps from within. The door slowly, stiffly creaked open. There, framed in the doorway, was the oldest man you could imagine, his grey beard reaching right down to his feet.

"Can you help me?" asked the boy. "I am looking for a place where no one ever dies."

"You have come to the right place," said the old man. "You have reached your journey's end. This indeed is the place where no one ever dies. This is the place where you can live forever. Come in, do. I would be glad of some company for I am here all alone." So he went into the castle and the great door swung to behind him.

At last the boy was content. Time passed. He and the old man kept each other company and many a tale was told between them.

One morning, when the sun rose and a slight breeze blew in through his bedroom window, he was suddenly reminded of the little bedroom where he had slept as a child and he was overcome by a great longing to see his own village again and to look into his mother's eyes. He wanted to see his whole family, his brothers and sisters, the neighbours — all the people who had shared his life, had comforted him in his troubles and had laughed and played with him in the sunshine.

He went to the old man and said, "Could you help me again? It is good being here with you but I would just like to have one look at the village where I was born and maybe pass the time of day with some of the neighbours and remind myself of my mother's face."

The old man frowned and said, "But you chose to come here. You chose the land where no one ever dies."

The boy sighed. "Just once I would like to go back. I really would like to see them. I'll come back when I've done."

"Very well. If that is your choice go to the stable, mount the white stallion and ride like the wind until you get back to your own village and then return. But take heed of this. Whatever happens, do not dismount. Stay on the horse until you are inside this castle once again, for if you put one foot on the earth you are doomed."

The boy did what he was told. He rode down the mountain road and off the way he had once travelled. Soon he came to a huge marsh and he saw nearby a heap of bones and a little pile of feathers. He realized that this was where there had once been a great sea, but the duck had long since drunk it dry. He did not get off his horse but rode on like the wind and soon came to a barren land where the wind tossed swirls of dust and an occasional dead stump pointed a wooden claw out of the ground. This had once been a green forest. He rode on and on. The land stretched flat and bare ahead with not a hill in sight. Once there had been a mighty mountain in those parts but it had been laid low and all its rocks and soil carried off in a wheelbarrow. At least he knew he was not far from home.

He came to a village where there was something familiar about the curve of the main street and the angle of a stream that ran beside it. Suddenly he realized that this was where his own village had once stood. But the stone houses had all gone and brick buildings replaced them. He turned his horse towards the lane where his own home used to be, but there was nothing of it to be seen but for a few scattered and broken blocks of stone. He rode back to the centre of the village. People passed him from time to time but their faces were unfamiliar and they did not look up at the boy on the big white horse. There was nothing for it but to go back the way he had come, so with a heavy heart he turned and galloped away from that place of strangers.

He rode hard, past the plain of rubble where there had once been a mountain, past the sandy desert where there had once been a forest and past the soggy marsh where the waves of the sea had once flowed towards the shore. When he reached the mountain road which led to the castle he could see ahead what seemed to be a cart with a lumpy load about halfway up the slope. He discovered when he reached it that it was tilted because one of its wheels had slipped down the mud into the ditch at the side of the road and an old man was vainly struggling to right the cart which was full of old boots and shoes. "Help me, please. It is nearly dusk and I cannot pull my cart out of the ditch before nightfall by myself," said the old fellow.

"I'm sorry, I cannot help you," replied the boy. "I have to stay on my horse."

"Oh, please have pity on an old man! Your limbs are young and strong. You could pull my cart back on the road in no time at all. What does one moment matter to someone who has all his life to come?"

Perhaps the man was right, thought the boy. After all, he had nothing but life ahead, so could surely spare a little of it now. He swung his leg over the horse's back and his foot touched the earth.

"Got you! Got you at last!" cried the man, gripping the boy by his wrist. "I have travelled the world looking for you. See all the boots and shoes I have worn out in my search? I am Death. No one escapes my clutch."

And the boy died there and then.

Two things stand out for me as I try to analyze the power of this story: the storyline (the events or "plot") and the underlying themes.

■ PLOT

"Plot" is what listeners fasten upon most readily and is what matters most, at least on the face of it. In this story the progress of the narrative in all its particulars is what occupies the attention from moment to moment. The listener, quite quickly, is presented with a quest towards an intriguing and fantastic goal, rather like the one which Prince Ivan pursued earlier when he left his father's palace, except that here we can sympathize more easily with the motivation (we would all like to pretend we are immortal!) and that strengthens the desire to know what will happen. I added the bit about the grandmother to the version I had heard in order to lock the boy's unlikely aim into a credible context. Having achieved the impossible, from his fantastic base the boy then sets out on a second quest. This is rather different in format from the norm of "questing" tales; yet, again like Prince Ivan, he retraces his journey out of love for his family and his home base. Such a spur can drive quite ordinary people in real life. It is an apparently viable aim.

When the boy arrives at the marsh, however, his new goal is immediately revealed to be at least as unattainable as the first. "What is going to happen next?" now makes room for a duality of expectation which adds to the attraction of the narrative. First, familiar ground is covered anew and the effects of the passage of centuries can be anticipated. But more important still is the knowledge that, as sure as night follows day, the boy will step down from his horse and he will meet his end — although the when and how of it occur unexpectedly (in spite of our wary anticipation of it), dramatically and swiftly.

Within these events the real and the extraordinary are constantly shifting places, merging, or staring each other in the face. I suspect that this process is closer than we realize to our own method of making sense of the world for ourselves. In reflecting upon past experience and anticipating the future, there is a tension between what actually happened and what might or should have happened, and between what it is reasonable to suppose will happen and what one fears or hopes will happen — the latter being particularly prone to pure fantasy. What I am suggesting is that there is some psychological rapport with this story because it follows the narrative pattern of normal human speculation.

Each significant event in the chain is visually distinct, yet not so clear-cut that the imagination becomes passively spongy. There is (for instance) an old man, his beard of defined length, a wheelbarrow with a certain load, a mountain with scree down one slope, and a small boy who stares. These separate and familiar elements combine to present an original and fanciful image; yet it is sufficiently restrained to allow the mind's eye room enough to invest the picture with additional specifics — colour, body, light and shade — upon the instant. This activity goes on, unrecorded, throughout the fun of listening, but here are two written examples (the boys were not asked to change the story in any way) that make the process explicit:

. . . he saw an old man pushing a wheelbarrow full of rocks. Mario stopped the old man. He noticed the long white beard and the eyes showing through the scraggy hair.

"Excuse me," said Mario. "I'm looking for the place where I can live forever."

The old man looked at Mario with a glint in his eyes. "Yes, my young friend, you have found the place. You see this enormous mountain behind me? Well by the time it takes me to carry piece by piece this mountain and dispose of it until there is nothing left, you would have lived an extremely long life."

Mario looked puzzled and asked the old man how long this would take . . .

John

He had walked several miles now and in the distance he could see an old man . . . Carlos stopped and looked at him. He was very small. His eyes were all bloodshot and he had a beard which reached his chest . . .

"You see those mountains over there?" said the old man. "Well, by the time we knock them down then you die." And suddenly appeared in front of him a large spade and a brown, rusty wheelbarrow . . .

Kevin S

The next two writers were in a class that was quite used to making what they wanted of a story told to them:

Eliza got very tired of walking so she rested on the ground. Then she saw an old man who was holding about eleven bricks in each hand.

"Please sir, do you know where there is a land where nobody will die forever?" asked Eliza.

"Oh yes, you are in the land already" said the old man.

"But how will I never die" she said.

"Oh, all you have to do is just with me bring the bricks from that mountain over there with grass on and bring them near to my house where there is a wall." . . .

Najma, aged ten

She came to an old woman with hair down to her waist . . . "Here it is. If you help take every pebble from this hill, after that only will you die." . . .

Lucy, aged ten

There is no reason to doubt that the examples above were visions which arose while listening to the account of the incident during the storytelling. The even flow of images in this story keeps the listener's imagination actively trapped to the end. How I remember being glued to the radio for the first broadcast of "Under Milk Wood" by Dylan Thomas: no stage or screen version of it since has busied my imagination to anything like the same degree.

■ THEMES

While narrative event comes directly to the inner eye, underlying themes, on the other hand, *covertly* envelope the spirit of the receiver. There is little or no reflection on events of the kind that, as in so many novels we could cite, actually dictates the reader's stance — which leaves enormous space for reflection to roam about just under the surface. I believe that the nature of the themes within "The Land Where No One Ever Dies" makes it an outstanding choice for the storyteller.

The boy pursues his unattainable ends with total commitment, in spite of warnings and scepticism from the old. Always appealing is the innocent child, naively chasing rainbows. The young like to hear about such a situation because they are in it; the old like to because they are wistful about it, while at the same time feeling oh, so wise and secure. When it comes to "universal themes" there are in fact relatively few that appeal equally to all age groups as this one does.

A second major source of reflection is the boy's desire to link up with his roots. We know about the urge to see again the place where we grew up, to discover what has changed and to hope for things to have remained the same. My head was filled with questions when I went back to my own patch of the Swansea valley a couple of years ago. Would I find the nooks and crannies of ancient hide-and-seek? The dark, dripping gully in the cliff by the railway track which turned into a fairy grotto in icicle time? Tiddlers and sticklebacks in the bend of the river by the play park? The hidden cave down the cwm, which was haunted? Would Ellis "Three-farthings" still be inside his draper's shop, not to mention the two Maggies, Sonti and Rangozzi, owners of rival ice cream parlours? And the Flats, fearsomely replete with fevers . . . etc., etc. Fascinating! But it was, as I might have known if I'd given the matter a thought, an ugly and boring place through the eyes of a Londoner who shall be nameless!

The boy is equally anxious to see his village again, and all who live there, an anxiety commonplace in the kitchens and living rooms of my pupils. It is a short step from there to the common curiosity about one's ancestors, whether an occasional tickle of interest or a burning need to know the maximum possible. The listener to this story will, therefore, sympathize with the boy's desire to return to his village.

More moving than any of this, however, is the dominant theme of the mutability of things. Everything that lives changes with time and is at last overcome. Whether one comes gently to terms with death or whether one "burns and raves" over "that good night," the inevitability of its approach and arrival is infinitely thought-provoking. Golden lads and chimney sweeps alike would surely be moved to hear a story based upon an attempt to escape the ravages of time.

To illustrate the effect it had on my 4's I will interpolate here a few of the poems written by the pupils during the course of follow-up work:

Time is a little boat blowing down a fast flowing river
When it comes to you and you let it go past
You can never get it back.

Time is a snowflake
By the time you are thinking what to do with it
It is gone.

Life is the dying sun in the evening
While you are enjoying it
It sinks into the horizon.

Life is a dying fire
At the moment it is still burning
By the next, it has died out.

           Kin Tai

Time
is a butterfly
fluttering past you.
You cannot catch it.
You cannot stop it.

           Jason

Time is essence
Time is life
Life is time

Time is like a long, long playtime
When you are born you come out and play
and play again
then — bang!
It's over.
You stand at the gates of time to live your next life.

Growing up is the sand of life.
Each grain of sand drops.
Your life is less and less each day
Until your sand has dropped for the last time.

Time
Time
is the shirt on my back:
The more you grow the less room you have;
Before you know it you've grown out of it
and your time has come to live among the dead.

                                        Errol

As time passes by
Leaves fall off the trees,
Turn gold and crispy
Go crunch when you tread on them.

Soon it will be Monday
Then Friday
The time goes by so quickly
You don't even notice.

My uncle An old, old man
Tells us how time passes so quickly.
He says
"A few years ago
I had to sweep dust from the chimney
But now
I am in a rocking chair,
Backwards
Forwards
Backwards."

                                Patrick

Time is passing
The trees lose their leaves
The winds from the North
start to blow up.
Skies are no longer clear blue
but cloudy.
As time passes
There is no sweet morning song
of the early bird.
Nor is there
the pleasant sound
of the busy bee
drinking
from the sweet smelling flower.

Time passes by
The snow begins
to paint
the ground
white.

Ricky

These, and many other thoughtful pieces like them, emerged from the felt experience of digesting the story, one which can hardly be described as action-packed. The most positive action is the boy's journeying, which is stated more than described as motion. Indeed, most of the "event" amounts to short bursts of conversation or brief, static descriptions of places where the "action" (the effect of the passage of time) has already taken place. Repetitions further reduce the potential excitement: the same — literal — ground is covered three times in all; then there is the "magic threesome" of old men differing one from another only by length of beard and the nature of their appointed tasks.

The fascination, therefore, is in the ideas. The action, such as it is, becomes the vehicle or symbol of the main theme. There is only one truly dramatic moment of the kind which would be deemed exciting to children if we were to take a conventional view of their tastes, and that comes at the very end. This is a tale which invites reflection. It is the sort of story that elicits the widest variety of successes in the classroom as far as I am concerned.

Nine

SELF-EXPRESSION
THROUGH STORY RETELLING

■ SHOSHANA'S STORY

At age four Shoshana told a story to her grandma who wrote it down:

A LITTLE GIRL, by Shoshana

One little girl that woke up this morning was happy. And she had a girl
friend and they were both happy. And they went home and napped. And then
they were happy and there was lots of toys and they played and played. The
next morning the whole world was happy. (That was a happy story, Grandma.
You know that!)

The Goodman Gazette, Vol 19, No 1, January 1987

It certainly was a happy story. And the chances are that the whole
world would be happy the next morning too, and the next, for a little girl
with Yetta Goodman for a grandma. Ken and Yetta Goodman of Tucson,
Arizona, are well known to British teachers of English for their work on the
miscue analysis of children's reading and for their "whole language"
approach to classroom activity. Of all the eminent gurus in the international
world of English teaching, none has appeared to me quite to match
Shoshana's grandma in wisdom and sunshine warmth. The last time we
met, Yetta was playing a guitar and singing folk songs, smiling, laughing
and easing others into singing themselves out of their reticences. Shoshana
is fortunate in having such roots. I would expect such a child to see the
world as a happy place and to compose correspondingly happy stories.

■ LOUISE'S STORY

Many children do not have this start in life. Over twenty-five years ago I cut out a short poem written by an eight-year-old girl called Louise, one which had been entered in a children's literary competition, and put the cutting into the wallet part of my purse. It is still with me today, many purses later and a bit more crumpled.

THE WIDE, WIDE WORLD

The world is wide
Theres no place to hide
There is no way out
I look round and about
I go to school everyday
And learn my sums the proper way.
Then when I go out to play I try to get out another way
But now I know theres no way out
All though I still look round and about.

People often react with, "An eight-year-old couldn't have written that!" If it's an English teacher speaking I immediately feel slightly tetchy. From others I understand the response and set about convincing them that an eight-year-old most certainly could, given a particular temperament and certain kinds of experiences. Of course, Louise was not one of my pupils and I know nothing about her apart from her name and her poem. Certainly it is not every eight-year-old who would have cause to see the world in this way; and other eight-year-olds sharing her view might not be blessed with either the occasion or the words to record it.

Not that there is anything technically special about the wording, which goes to show what a lot of nonsense it is for linguists and grammarians and ministers of education to claim that you can't be properly literary without self-conscious complexity of sentence structures and a great big vocabulary to match. A high proportion of the vocabulary is monosyllabic, and simple main clauses predominate. But it is a piece of literature. She put her small finger on the very centre of human depression. Succintly, movingly, simply, she says that there seems no way out of hopelessness when one is in it up to the neck, in spite of the limitless resources of the outside world. Auden's bereaved mourner in "Funeral Blues" cannot stop the clocks, silence the telephone, or cause the busy world to pause for so much as a moment to acknowledge the outrage of the tragedy. Ill luck is no respecter of persons.

I remember in the course of the narrative-charged TV reporting of the 1987 Zeebrugge ferry disaster a voice telling of a little girl who, it was claimed, protested that she didn't deserve to drown because "I've been good and never told anyone lies." Later she was rescued. It's all there, in the poem. I wouldn't have understood it at the age of eight when, book thieves aside, life was jolly, but by the time I had reached the age Louise should have reached by now her message could not have been more apt — but that's another story.

And what has all this to do with storytelling? Just this: self-expression is often cited as an essential component of children's education, but not a lot of what a child does in the classroom actually demands very much of it. I've seen a fair amount of sameness in pupil output, and even art rooms appear to say more of the teacher than the pupils. By contrast, story retelling releases the writer's individuality, often to an extraordinary degree. So here is my hypothesis: *storytelling and story retelling allow a child's view of the world to emerge, safely.*

A look back at "The Land . . ." through the eyes of several retellers will illustrate what I mean. First I must face the unanswerable question: "What is self — that self which we want to have expressed — anyway?" There is no reason, here, to be too clever over this. For the moment I am concerned with two elements. One is temperament — the propensity to be especially cheerful, loving, reflective, grumpy, fearful, impatient, greedy, sympathetic, resourceful, long-suffering, impulsive, persistent or whatever, which, if differences in the natures of siblings brought up in a shared environment is anything to go by, may well be inside human creatures at their embryonic start. The other is the day after day accumulation of experiences and activities which add up to form a person's own culture. The two work on each other, moulding, modifying, directing, and increasingly the individual is free-willed (or free-wheeled) into individuality. Into identity. Into "the self."

Next I shall focus a little on the retellers themselves. I feel as if I could write a whole book about the point I am making in this section, just using retellings of "The Land . . ." I shall play safe here, however, and limit my illustrations to three.

■ KEVIN

I taught Kevin English for a total of three years and got to know him quite well — insofar as an English teacher can when there are about a hundred and fifty young people to engage with in the course of any one year. From the beginning it was clear that he had more than a touch of a Shoshana about him. You'll see what I mean, perhaps, from something he wrote soon after he arrived at the school:

Barbados is a wonderful place. We went on the sea shore. The beach was lovely. My grandmother was nice but I didn't understand her. She had one leg and I wondered why she had one leg then my dad's sister gave us rice and peas. It was nice. Then we went out on a walk. This man on a bicycle was selling snowballs which are drinks with crushed ice in. I had one. It was cold . . .

Then we went to a house. It was my step-sister's mum's house. I had not seen my step-sister. She was eighteen years old. I kissed her. We went to get some snowballs . . .

One road had a cut in it where dirty water went. I liked it. It looked nice but was dirty . . .

My dad's friend worked on a ship. I went on the ship. I liked it. The people looked friendly when we went into town. It was like Wood Green but there were no cars . . .   The police wear black trousers with a red stripe and with a white jacket and hat on.

Inside that writer nestled a generous spirit. A few bouts of furious aggression during his early secondary school years, always as a result of some severe provocation, misled one or two of his teachers in their assessment of him. But these were exceptions to the rule of a cheerful, appreciative and loving disposition. He was the product of a secure and supportive home. Usually quiet in class, when discussion bubbled and frothed around him he would listen for a long time before venturing in, invariably to make a significant and thought-provoking shift in the flow. His "self" gleamed out of his written work increasingly. Here are some extracts from his first second-year piece of work, composed a bit less than a year after the above:

The best moments were when I played out. Sometimes we went to the shopping city [a shopping mall in Wood Green, the nearest one to Tottenham] — that was good. We played He - one, two. I went through the shopping hall. No one was there. Up the stairs through C and A I saw Mark and caught him. It got boring so I went home and watched TV. "Mosschop" was on — that was good . . .

Next day, me, mum, Karen and Dad went to the sea side. It takes three hours . . .   We had lunch when we got there at twelve — sandwiches and rice and meat and sweets and coke. It was lovely. I ate till I was full, so did everyone . . .   I went in the sea. Only my feet went in — it was cold . . .

Next week was the week before school. We went to the pictures and saw the star film. That was good. After that we went to the chip shop. I bought a pie which was nice . . .

Next day I went to Wood Green. I bought a shirt and cords, blue. I ironed them when we went home. Everything was done, I could not wait for school . . .

As time went on, Kevin's thoughtful side began to emerge in his written work while his outgoing warmth still established the tone:

ME

My mind is like two people, Do and Don't. Don'ts good and Do's bad. If I have
not done my homework Do will say
"say you've nearly done it"
But Don't will say
"Do it now for tomorrow"

[*Enter Launcelot Gobbo, stage left!*]

But me, I really like quiet when I'm in my bed, just looking at the wall. I
can think.

I really like parties or dances because of the music and the bass. I like the
feel of it — it goes through you, and the food is very nice too.

I really hate the news on telly. All you hear is about bombs and war all
over the world. Also I really hate people who shoot foxes. I think it is very cowardly to shoot a poor little fox. How would the hunters like foxes to destroy
their children? I think people like that are nuts.

I like it when something is wrong. I can talk to my mum. She would listen
to me and then she would tell me what I should do.

I like it when I'm with my friend. We can talk about things. If I had no
friend I would not be happy.

There was a whole range of demands being made on 2/C at that
time, and they were not always asked to deliver introspective, personal
compositions. I have selected these particular pieces because they give
some insight into the character of one pupil and show how it affects his
story retelling. Even when he is expected to look objectively outwards, the
essential Kevin is still there. Here he is writing about his neighbours, a
topic in which my teaching practice experience had provided me with
enormous faith.

I live on a very quiet road. Some of the people on our streeet keep
themselves very much to themselves . . .

On our side of the street lives Michael and his family. I like Michael's
mum and dad — they really are fun people and me and Michael are the best
of mates . . .

At the end of our street lives the mad lady. She's old and talks to herself
very loudly. You hardly see her but sometimes boys go and throw stones at her
window . . .

But me and my mates go and hang around the flower park. You can sit and
think and tell jokes and talk. Around our area the people are very kind and
happy. I think if someone moved in they would fit in just like a puzzle. I would
hate it if I had to move.

The style of that last paragraph gives an indication of the progress Kevin had been making, albeit slowly, during his first two years. But the following three pieces illustrate a spectacular leap forward.

JOY

What gives me joy is when the sky is blue and the
sun is bright yellow, and when the grass is green
That is when I want to go out and play in the fields.

We read and discussed a lot of poems in the week immediately after the composition of "Joy." Kevin responded thoughtfully to all the new material, and because he was such a patient and empathetic listener, the effect on his own work was very evident. The next two poems he wrote precisely one week later:

MY BIKE

Riding far and wide on the road
watching men go down manholes, women
with babies do the shopping,
cars moving slow in jams . . .
Out of the town
and into the countryside!
Jump over the golden river!
The sun setting in the west
and me to ride home.

THE NEW STAR

Through the sky I see a star sparkling
Sisters scattered all around,
Spinning, slipping
Not a star but a star ship moving
at light speed, slipped into
a time wrap and never to come back.

He hasn't changed essentially, just grown — and, of course, acquired skills en route.

Now let me move straight on to his fourth year and present the first half of his version of "The Land . . ." Beamed out to Kevin was a story that was essentially about not wanting to die. In response he wrote one about wanting to be alive, reminding me about what John Berger wrote in a publication based upon the TV version of the story:

[*The story is*] about the human desire to discover or invent strategies for outwitting time. The young man in the fable tries to cheat death . . .

A need for what transcends time, or is mysteriously spared by time, is built into the very nature of the human mind and imagination. One has to live with this need without deceiving oneself.

About Time

There is an important difference in Kevin's story. His hero, Peter, is thinking about living, not dying. He constantly reminds the reader of the riches of life in a way that no other retelling I have received has done — whether from ten-year-olds, from other 4's, from a group of adults at a conference, or from mature students in our locality. Only Kevin changed the tone and message into a veritable celebration of life.

I must draw attention to two other significant features of his story. First, Peter's roots are in a loving home and his mother weeps to part with her son, just as one day, perhaps, Kevin's mother will when he finally leaves the nest. I would if he were mine! Second, Peter sorrows for the old men in the story and, just as his creator would, offers sympathy and practical assistance. Yet inside himself neither the fictional nor the real-life boy can come to terms with the negativism so alien to each: therefore he moves on in the narrative.

Knowing what I do of Kevin, I would claim his writing to be a high-powered piece of self-expression, inextricably linked to his own temperament and his own view of the world. He identifies and underpins something of himself in the act of writing, as he likely would in other self-expressive things in art, crafts, humanities, social studies, etc. Who would doubt that he gains in self-knowledge through the writing?

■ KEVIN'S STORY

Peter looked round and loved what he saw. His mother gave him breakfast with her loving smile. He wondered why people killed each other. He wondered why some people had money and others didn't. Just then his father walked into the kitchen. "Good morning," said his dad. Peter just kept looking sadly out of the kitchen window. "Today, Peter, stay at home. You don't look too well." Peter only looked up and finished his breakfast.

From his house he could see the mountain in the distance. He thought it was magnificent with its snow capped top gleaming in the sun. This made him feel much happier. He had better get dressed and go out, he thought. That afternoon made him feel so happy it occurred to him that things could be like this forever. He sat in the shade of the apple tree sipping his drink. How, he wondered, could he live for ever. The idea was still on his mind at tea time. He told his mum that he must go away and find a way to live for ever.

He set out sadly but confidently leaving his confused mum at the gate, weeping. He assured her that he would be alright but she still cried.

On his travels he met an old bent-backed man emptying a wheelbarrow. Peter greeted him but in reply the old man gave Peter only a cold stare. Peter asked the old man if he wanted any help. The old man looked sharply at Peter and said "All I want is to die and I cannot die until this mountain is completely pulled down."

"Why do you want to die?" Peter asked in reply. The old man said "I have lived for hundreds of years and am all alone and I just want to die and I cannot die until I've pulled down this mountain with my bare hands." Peter tried to cheer up the old man but failed.

He left to set off along the dusty road on his tiresome task but he hadn't been travelling long when he met another old man in a forest. This was the most magnificent forest Peter had ever seen. Its trees were all different shades of green. He could hear bees and little creatures and birds chirping happily in the woods. All this made Peter feel relaxed and happy. He sat on a log and looked up at the sunlight streaming through the branches. He turned back to the second old man. This old man had a pruning fork [*pruning knife!*]. He didn't look very happy Peter thought. I wonder why — "Goodday" he smiled. The old man looked up "Who are you?" "My name is Peter." Peter then picked a strawberry off a bush. He noticed the second old man looked less happy than the first. "What's the matter?" Peter asked. The old man replied crossly "I have to cut down the forest and it is going to take two hundred years." Peter felt sorry for the old man but set off.

After many, many years Peter came to a big, big ocean. He could see in the sea the golden fins flashing in the sun light. As the sun light hit the water it made it glitter and glisten. Peter loved it. On the shore was a third old man. This one had long grey hair and under his arm was a golden duck. Peter walked over and sat on the soft sand. "Hello" called Peter. "Go away" the old man shouted back. He looked at Peter and said "I have to make this duck drink all the ocean before I can die."

Peter decided to leave the old man so he said "Goodbye." The old man didn't even look at Peter leave. Peter had set off a third time. After the three encounters Peter was still determined to live forever. Then just as he was setting up camp for the night he glimpsed the shadowy silhouette of a castle nearby.

When he awoke he could see the beautiful castle and all its colourful flags flying in the brisk wind. Peter knew this was what he was looking for. He ran happily up to the great heavy drawbridge. It lowered for him. A young man dressed in white was waiting for him. The young man said "We know you want to live for ever so come and stay with us." Peter was overjoyed. In the castle there was nothing to tell the time. In the castle Peter and his friend danced, they sang the whole of the day.

There's a lot to be said for the Shoshanas and Kevins of this world. My husband and I once happened to see Kevin in a shopping centre with another lad I didn't know — maybe his neighbour, Michael. He didn't see us until they were almost past, then he stopped stock still in his tracks. Apart from an "Oh, hello, miss" he was — oddly, I thought — quite speechless, but beaming from ear to ear. He could have hurried on, or even pretended he hadn't seen a teacher at all, but instead he just stood and glowed with wordless pleasure, apparently prepared to remain there indefinitely.

That sort of recognition puts you in a good mood. Like going to my butcher's down the road, the best butcher's shop in north London. It's run by two Greek brothers and their assistant, Fred, whose shock of silver hair I can see from the other side of the street even if he's in the back of the shop. They invent and invite stories in there, and they are always, always smiling. "How was Holland, then?" when I've just come back from Bergen-on-Sea; "How's the diet, then?" when my husband's doing an exclusive fish, veg and the ubiquitous soya bean (not much fun for the butcher's till!); "How's the book going? Are we in it?" I say "Of course!" and we all laugh — they think I'm joking. I really hate the chops and mince on soulless supermarket shelves!

In the matter of foodstuffs, when Kevin was little he was somewhat round in build — perhaps because of plenty of good West Indian rice and peas. He grew to be a tall 5, but his disposition remained as plump and well-nourished as ever.

■ ELROY

Elroy, my next subject, had a decidedly lean and hungry look which emanated not from the body but from the spirit. Unlike Kevin, who wanted to be in school, Elroy was more often elsewhere. He arrived somewhere towards the end of the second year, from (so he told us) the Bronx of New York, and stayed to the middle of the fourth. And I don't think he left us for an alternative educational establishment.

He was very different from Kevin. Almost as soon as he joined 2/C I had him seated on my desk at the front to talk to everyone, with the class ranged round him much as they had congregated round Abit's rendering of his very first piece of work in the English language, and round lots of other readers, talkers and tale-tellers before and since. He liked the attention but had the wisdom not to exploit it: in his descriptions of his experiences in New York he only hinted at confrontations with flick-knives and was not invited either by me or by anyone else to provide details. I only caught whiffs of a family. He lived, it seemed, with his mother and brothers, but his father . . .? Perhaps in New York. He once mentioned an uncle. I saw a brother once or twice round about the school gates, a good deal older than Elroy, much bigger, and I could have felt a bit afraid but that I would instantly rattle on about his being the spitting image of his little brother, wasn't he? (big grin) — which would disarm him, making it easier for me to encourage him to move off. Elroy was something of a loner at school, but outside, it was said that he spent much of his time with that older brother and . . . companions. Elroy's retelling was, needless to say, totally different from Kevin's, giving very different messages. I know he enjoyed doing it because he actually took it home to finish.

■ ELROY'S STORY

One day there was a boy named Mike. He was sixteen years old and had left school with good qualifications. He was very fond of his dad Mike and his dad used to go driving in a convertible seven series BMW. They go to the park play some football and sit down and smoke and have a nice time and Mike would go swimming with his friends if his dad didn't feel like going swimming. One day his father didn't want to go swimming so Mike went swimming with his friends and had a nice time so after the swimming Mike came home his mum was in the front room crying with her next door neighbour and she told Mike that his father is in hospital very sick and almost dying so he started crying. After five minutes there was a knock on the door it was inspector Finigan saying that Mike's dad would like to see Mike and his wife at the hospital so they got their coats and went into the car and drove down there. They had reached the hospital and Mike's dad said I love you but I have to go soon Mike said what do you mean your going not thinking what he meant. He went to his wife take care of my son and said I love you too and she gave him a kiss and he died when she gave him a kiss. So after that they came home and Mike said is there anywhere I can live for ever mum she started to laugh a bit so Mike said I don't care anyway because I know there is a place where I can live for ever I'm packing my clothes and leaving tomorrow. It was getting late and he finished packing so he went to his bed. As time went by he was still sleeping then he woke up and got washed put on his clothes he took his bank book and change out his money and took his dads BMW and drove it on his journey. As he was driving he met an old man with a white beard he asked the man if you can tell me where I could find the land where I could live forever May be over there in the mountains but that would take you one hundred years so he got into the car and carried on driving as he was driving he saw some man with a long white beard that came down to his chest so Mike asked him where can I live for ever the old man said if you look over there there is a big forest and in the middle of it there is a place where you can live for ever so he got into his car and started driving. As he reached half way the car conked out so he got out of the car got his bags and began walking he walked and walked it began getting dark but he still kept on walking. Finally he came to the palace and he knocked on the door and an old man came to the door with a long white beard come down to his knees so Mike asked him is this the palace where I can live forever the old man said yes yes come in what is your name my name is Mike what's yours mine is Steve sit down are you hungry. As days went by they did get on well together they smoked together drink talk and played cards with each other. And Mike showed Steve the games he played where he grew up and one day Mike said to Steve you remind me of my dad.

That's it, in full. In the process of impressing his own person upon his version, he ended it where he wished it to end. I checked: it wasn't simply that he gave up at that point, having already produced such an uncharacteristically vast amount of writing. And that's where I end my public reflections upon the lad I have called Elroy. There is nothing more in his exercise book because he left, without our having the chance to tell him how interesting and different we found his retelling of this tale.

■ EARL

The next one says something about a very specific and vital cultural feature: language. Earl (remember Earl and his chatty Pelops who sat swigging nectar with grandad Zeus?) cheerfully revealed to me his pride in his West Indian roots. I am reasonably confident he would have participated in patois speech at home and in the company of an uncle, the sleeves of whose reggae records sometimes decorated the classroom walls. This speech would have been somewhat different again from the so-called London Jamaican which has jelled around most of the black youth of the metropolis, but which is also, increasingly, becoming incorporated into the repertoire of young people of very different ethnic origins, including some indigenous cockneys.

I use the word *repertoire* advisedly. There is a mistaken view held by some that the speech (and therefore the potential to write) of working class children is by nature restricted. This is not so in my experience, either when they are using their most familiar, comfortable forms, or at other times when the need to use a different dialect or register arises. Earl, whose retelling I shall be quoting here, was perfectly capable of producing a serious piece in standard English which was his usual classroom medium:

THE SCREAM

There she was
walking
with hen short
feeble
legs struggling,
carrying her small body
along the wooden pier
which is being
eaten away
by
the dark grey sea,
the same sea
as the dull grey

sky.
And a strong
blistering wind
is making the sea
rough,
tugging the boats
in the background
harder
and harder
making each anchor
strain to hold
on to
the bottom
of the grey sea.
The woman stumbled
on
past two lovers
walking
hand in hand.
She studies them
as they pass her.
What was she
thinking?
As she looked back
she saw
what she feared.

A little boy
was standing
on the top of the pier boundary
looking like he wanted to jump.
No, little boy,
No!

She screamed.

Earl began as an uncertain performer when written work was required and would be constantly demanding assistance, often more out of fear of failure than actual incompetence. He loosened up as time went on and was at his liveliest when tapping the resource of his dialect. Let me add that there was never any question of his white Anglo English teacher presuming to "teach" black dialect. All I did was to make clear that I considered it no less respectable and expressive than any other dialect (including written standard, which I teach all the time, as all English teachers do as part of their normal job) and to that end would incorporate the services of dialect performers, both pupil and professional, into the lessons. As I have stated in an earlier section, there was plenty of literature by black writers in classroom and cupboard. Black dialect and reggae rhythms are as much a part of Earl's culture as Clydach, Sospan Fach, Dylan Thomas, choral singing, words like "twp" and a Welsh accent are part of mine; any attempt to pluck it all out would be crippling.

■ EARL'S STORY

Here is the opening part of Earl's story, heavily influenced by his linguistic background:

"Mum, mum where granma, mum, where gran?" said Nick coming in from playing with his friend all day. "I've got somethink to show her."
"She gone . . ."
"Gone where?"
"She dead . . ."
"Dead? When? How?" said Nick.
"She die today a couple of hour ago."
"No, no, no it can't be!"
Nick went up to his granma room and started to cry on her. "Granma, please get up, please, please." Nick started to cry even more. He went down stairs crying still and asked his mum, "Mum, is they a place where I could live for ever, a place that never end?"
Nick mum started to giggle and said, "They is no such place where you can live forever, there is only one place and that is heaven up above where the great god is: Jah, Rasta four eye, you know."
"No, there is a place. I can feel it in my heart and my soul. There is a place . . ."

■ OTHER STORIES

Self-expression is not only affected by temperament and cultural (in the broadest sense) background. Intelligence is a component to which I have made little reference in selecting examples, either here or in other sections. There is no substitute for it, after all! Most people, in trying to assess the value of a stimulus to writing in an English lesson, would be looking for a revelation of outstanding talent in the results. For some, in the context of Arts education, intelligence is synonymous with talent, with creative originality, and they might even be tempted into imagining that the only self-expression which matters is the clever kind. I believe that all kinds of self-expression are significant to a child's development and to anyone's peace of mind.

I need hardly state at this stage that I am not particularly concerned with a comparison of talents, but with variety instead. Furthermore, because the most talented pupil always emerges as such even when the classroom stimulus is unremarkable, I have not put myself out here to draw attention to the fact that there were, among my pupils, natural storytellers, gifted individuals who came into their own during the course of this work. Some did. There were inevitably, too, the very able pupils who positively excelled themselves. Alas, much of the "best" work has disappeared into the vaults of the Joint Matriculation Board in the north of England.

I want to leave the precincts of my own classrooms for a moment. A truth is the more true when one's own experience is confirmed by the experience of others.

I attended a workshop in London in early 1987. The workshop brief ran as follows:

Stories from Stories: Mike Hill and Colleagues
(Terriers Middle School, High Wycombe)

Teachers from the school are active participants in the London Narrative Group. They have tapes, transcripts, etc. of the retelling of stories by pupils. A central interest is the ways in which retellers change stories in the telling and what these changes signify. Of particular interest is retelling by second language learners.

Mike, the headteacher, and his colleagues Linda and Angela, ran the most inspiring conference workshop that I have ever attended anywhere. The mass of living testimony exchanged among the twenty or so participants and the group leaders was quite overwhelming. Such a short while before, at another London conference, teachers were asking, "How do you do it? How do you get started? Will it work? Should I . . .? Could I . . .?" That was when I wrote the article that became chapter six. And some time before that I had attended a conference devoted exclusively to narrative, where (or so it seemed to me) many of the participants had hardly grasped that oral narrative existed on the educational horizon at all, never mind its having a classroom place. There appeared to have been a staggering turnaround in a matter of two and a half years.

In 1987 discussion centred on what was released in child narratives. There was ample mention of talent among the obviously gifted school achievers, but what people got most excited about was the unsuspected hidden talent which is liberated through retellings. Quite spectacular evidence of follow-up progress on the part of pupils was put before our eyes.

Anwara, a solitary Bengali speaker among English and/or Punjabi speakers, would relate to no one except the Special Needs teacher (and the hamsters!), much to the distress of Linda, her mainstream teacher, for whom she appeared to have no English whatsoever. Until, that is, a flurry of story times enabled the silent Anwara to retell a story to the tape recorder, in which she gave vent to a command of English which astounded all the adults who knew her. Photocopies of her subsequent written work were then put before us, beginning with the first piece of writing she ever produced shoulder to shoulder with her classmates, which amounted to five lines about a pink mug, and on to almost as many pages of her retelling of Linda's (told) version of a portion of *Macbeth* — with less than four months between the two!

The opportunity to retell a story told by the teacher had similarly startling results in the case of Asid in Angela's class who, until that phase of his school life began, had been an unusually slow ESL learner.

We also heard from a teacher of traveller children who apparently think nothing of their own extraordinary talents as storytellers: such pupils deserve ample opportunity to display their prowess, given their otherwise low status.

There are those who, like Elroy, benefit from the chance to express some fundamental needs and desires through retelling, given apparent freedom from the constraint of having to invent a storyline. We heard of several during the workshop: a black child turned a splendid fairytale monarch into a black king; three girls in Angela's class who heard my telling of "The Land . . ." each made the main character female; Dennis (of Abit's story) needed his happy ending.

An enormous area for exploration is the extent to which prejudice, and its opposite, are given voice in the retelling of stories. A primary school teacher from central India referred to a story she tells her classes which is from an area of southern India as different culturally from her own place of origin as the Western Isles of Scotland are from the centre of Birmingham. She comes to the class armed with actual costumes and artifacts from the region to provide a backcloth to the telling. Subsequent retellings by pupils often contain deliberate links with the place of the story's birth, which might otherwise be located in a geographical and cultural vacuum by teacher and pupils alike — along with many a child of overseas origin. Such evidence of intercultural awareness is precious.

Another major bonus focused upon was that children, when orally retelling a story told first by the teacher, often reveal and extend their social orientation. With the aid of tapes and transcripts, Mike and his colleagues showed how their children could collaborate: approval flits back and forth between a responsive audience and a talented young performer, while a hesitant one launches himself anew on the strength of his listeners' promptings, which are sometimes voiced but more often silently mouthed. There were pairs and small groups of children who worked together to finish up with entertaining and dramatic tapes; the occasional child clearly felt free to use the process to establish his or her own status within the peer group.

The best moment of that workshop was hearing Angela say that though she had to muster her courage to tell rather than read a story to her class, it was marvellously worthwhile: "There is an exhilaration about it.

You can never look back but only go forward once you've done it." These are the words of someone who knows how to be happy in her work! Like Shoshana. Like Kevin.

How could I doubt that my own storytelling helped me to know Kevin, Elroy and Earl, to name but three, and helped them to come to terms with themselves?

Ten

BACKUP MATERIAL FOR STORYTELLING

I doubt if the idea of a term's work based around storytelling would ever have entered my head but for a chance to bring "The Land Where No One Dies" and my favourite class together. Normally 4's, 5's and 6's — which were all I would see during that year — met a dose of coursework, essay assignments and projects, and the sharing of literature was largely for the same examination purposes. But with that class there would be room for a little deviation for the enjoyment of hearing some good stories.

It was August 1985, at our retreat in a little Wiltshire village, that I put my mind to the nitty-gritty of the next academic year. Administrative and prepare-for-exams demands would make it a year of hard craft. There was the one consolation that at least one of my teaching groups would contain familiar, friendly faces. Initially I thought I would spend half an hour or so of my first lesson with 4/C just telling them "The Land . . ." for our mutual pleasure and as a way to establish swiftly our old terms of reference; then I would get down to the real work! But even as I contemplated this there was a certain discomfort at the back of my head: hadn't I discovered with "The King Who Promised" and other tales told to junior classes that storytelling was not just a sideline culled from the precincts of the toddler's bedside and the primary school? Would such a brief one-off not be a waste?

At the very least I could ponder the themes for a while in the good company of Hakan, Che, Chris and all the rest. Were there any poems and stories from the various sample anthologies I'd brought with me into the country which would offer good follow-up material? Another real favourite of mine was the Orpheus myth which was not all that far away: here, too, was a refusal to accept impotence in the face of humankind's mortality.

And so the whole idea took shape. "The Land . . ." would be introduced at the start of term. Sometime later it would be joined by Orpheus and Eurydice. And in between, as many stories as I could dig up which would create the world of Hades in the heads of 4/C. What a great idea! But what about my other fourth-year class, 4/R, all strangers to me? I hesitated to begin storytelling with a pack of sceptical fifteen-year-olds, but longterm story work would mean masses of preparation and it would have to do for both groups. Well, it had to be done. It had to be done! Why should 4/C be favoured and 4/R deprived?

Soliloquies of this kind in the peace of the English country summer helped me to muster all my courage to storytell to upper secondary classes. This meant the daring business of abandoning texts, a process which I described in some detail in chapter five.

But once the story was told there would be texts. Having spent all my teaching years extending my pupils through literature, there was no question of suddenly casting aside tried and trusted friends. Over the years, centre stage for lessons had included drama, media study, the analysis of language and dialect, integrating music and drama, and so on in secondary schools, and a range of environmental and scientific projects in primary schools. All of them inevitably involved speculation; and literature was usually available to fortify it. Though it appeared to me by then that an oral story was the single most effective means of plundering the first classroom resource, the children, literature still remained indispensable. I am sceptical of English lessons which draw from the pupils without feeding in anything of literary substance, however punchy the worksheets may appear. It is as unproductive as a dependence upon printed texts without reference to the experience of the pupils. Both are likely to elicit superficial, unfelt or secondhand written work. So, first I would select backup texts with which to surround the stories I wanted to tell.

In addition to the first and last of the set, I would include stories associated with the tormented spirits — Ixion, Tantalus, Sisyphus and any others I fancied and could find out about. Then there were those connected with Hades himself and the running of his realm: Persephone (she was a must), Charon and perhaps Cerberus. We scoured the bookshops of Devizes and Marlborough for both volumes of Graves's *The Greek Myths* and I decided the chief characters from that. Having established the emphasis I would give to each story or set of stories, I set about browsing through books for suitably supportive prose and poetry, a pleasant, leisurely occupation.

First I mulled over the already mentioned themes of my opening tale. Nostalgia for the homeland figured first — a significant feature in the lives of the immigrant parents and grandparents of my London-born, multi-ethnic pupils.

I remember back home
Sky blue
Sea clean
Sun warm and radiant
Looking at himself in the water
Glittering and shining in the morning waves . . .

Donald Peters

These were the very first words I read in my search, right
at the beginning of the *Caribbean Anthology* (produced by the Inner
London Educational Authority's own publishing centre).

In "Flame-heart" Jamaican writer Claude McKay describes how
memories become hazy and distorted. Vivid recollections cease to be
attached to dates and seasons:

I have forgot the special, startling season
Of the pimento's flowering and fruiting;
What time of year the ground doves brown the fields
And fill the noon day with their curious fluting . . .

The poet finds that he has:

. . . embalmed the days
Even the sacred moments when we played
All innocent of passion, uncorrupt,
At noon and evening in the flame-heart's shade.

It is the "flame" of the poinsettia, "red, blood red, in warm December" which
he can place most exactly.

Here was a chance to catch something of the West Indies in the
classroom and then to draw out of my pupils equally precise recollections
from their own past lives. I would get them to write some poems about
them. There was no shortage of autobiographical prose and poetry for such
a purpose — one is spoilt for choice!

Amongst the material I had on hand was a perfect little piece by James
Berry, who had worked in our school and become a good friend. It was a
poem in the guise of a conversation between a child and her nagging
parent, pestering as to why she had shot off to her grandmother's house:

Wha mek yu go Granny Yard?
   Mi go Granny Yard
   fi go get sorrel drink.
An dat a really really true?
   Cahn yu hear a true?
Yu noh did go fi notn else?
   Dohn yu hear a nota else?

Sorrel drink is delicious — at least the liquid I made according to the instructions in my Jamaican cookery book was. I came across the basic ingredient — wine-pink flowers of sorrel *(hibiscus sabariffa)* — at my favourite West Indian greengrocer's in Wood Green one December. Apparently it is a favourite choice for visitors who pop in during the Christmas season. In the course of the poem, the child gathers all sorts of goodies from granny — lemonade, orange wine, boiled pudding, ginger cookies, coconut cake — but eventually the real reason for her visit, the something else, is winkled out:

Wha mek yu go Granny Yard?
    Mi go Granny Yard
    fi go hide from punishment.
Fi go hide from punishment?
    Fi go hide from punishment.

This poem, as I anticipated during the planning of the work, led to a lot of talk in the classroom about the various means of ensuring a comforting sanctuary from the hot seat, and grandparents figured large yet again as they had a long time before when Abit had first read to everyone in Turkish; and a granny had had a significant place, too, in the upbringing of the boy who wanted to live forever.

Another Jamaican poet, Dennis Scott, personified time to useful effect from my point of view when it came to the theme of mutability:

Uncle Time is a ole, ole man . . .
All year long 'im wash 'im foot in de sea
long, lazy years on de wet san'
and shake de coconut tree dem
quiet-like wid 'im sea-win' laughter,
scrapin' away de lan'

Uncle Time is a spider-man, cunnin' and cool . . .

Like Anansi, Time progresses surreptitiously. He offers the bitter bread of grief:

Watch how 'im spin web roun' you house, an creep
inside; an' when 'im touch yu, weep.

Nearer to the children's own approach was "Time" by Edward Brathwaite, which begins:

Time is the grey wood
streaked with grain
tears carve a trail down its grave pain . . .

And there were other poems which went down well, even including one which dealt directly with death: I quoted earlier in chapter six extracts from "To my mother," a really moving poem by E.M. Roach which occupied a good half-hour of one September lesson. Death is a tricky subject in a locality which is short of neither violent incidents nor those serious illnesses which associate themselves with poverty. Some pupils have seen more of death than I have, so one treads warily if at all, using samples — like the Roach poem — which are safely distant in their particulars (though not necessarily in feelings and attitudes) from anything the pupils may have personally encountered. Several other poems were just read aloud by somebody once or twice. When it seemed productive to linger and dig deep, that's just what happened, often in small group discussions first. Afterwards the different feelings and interpretations elicited within the safety of the few would be pooled for everybody's consideration.

Poetry seemed to me to be the most evocative vehicle for thoughts about time and its consequences. But sharing the sights and sounds, fears and fun, of early childhood should prove a wordy business, so I would look out for some good passages of prose to jog their memories and help them along the language routes. There are no page references for these in my summer vacation notes — I simply dug into my memorized repertoire of useful incidents from various novels and autobiographies and scribbled a reminder. Even before I picked up my pen for this purpose I could see at least three weeks of work taking shape round the first of my stories alone: a week for the straight retellings, a week or more of poetry reading/writing and mulling over the work produced during the first week, and a week for recalling early childhood — perhaps to include a visit from the parent of one of the pupils — and
recording that in prose or poetry.

My ideas for Orpheus and Eurydice would last even longer. A whole term could be taken up with stories, there was no doubt about it. And the backup texts I found for those stories were numerous.

I won't list every one — choices are very much a matter of personal taste and knowledge anyway — but simply offer a sample, staying with "The Land . . .," my version, based on the one that is included in Italo Calvino's collection of Italian folk tales.

They ranged geographically from ancient Greece with Virgil's *The Georgics* to works by young contemporary West Indian writers and, as far as this soil is concerned, back to ancient Britain with Beowulf, to Shakespeare and on to the present poet laureate. I used prints of paintings, drawings and lithographs, and when it came to Orpheus, tapes of music by a few of the many composers who have themselves been inspired by the story.

■ THREE WEEKS PLUS

Themes
Aspiration/actuality; longing for birthplace; inevitability of change/death.

Texts

1. Poems	Donald Peters

I remember back home	
Flame-heart	Claude McKay
I remember	Hugh Boatswain
I remember, I remember	Thomas Hood
South	Edward Brathwaite
Skating bit from "The Prelude"	Wordsworth
Mi go Granny Yard	James Berry
Sunny Market Song	James Berry
Uncle Time	Dennis Scott
Autobiographical Note	Vernon Scannell
Time	Edward Brathwaite
Fear no more the heat o' the sun	Shakespeare
To my Mother	E.M. Roach
The Wind in the Dooryard	Derek Wilcott

(etc. as chosen by pupils from various anthologies)

2. Prose	Frank O'Connor

My Oedipus Complex	
Infant school bits from "Cider with Rosie"	Laurie Lee
Grandfather bits in "Portrait of the Artist"	Dylan Thomas
Grandmother bits in "My Childhood"	Gorky
Tar bubbles, "There Is a Happy Land"	Keith Waterhouse
Tadpoles in wellies, "Kestrel for a Knave"	Barry Hines
Catching carp, in "A Bit of Bread and Jam" from The Goalkeeper's Revenge	Bill Noughton

Week One:

Tell story; oral and written retellings by pupils.

Week Two:

1. Pairs/groups listing precious moments from the past — physical detail of occasions, people, favourite things, places . . . Get parents to make lists too; lists made up in conjunction with brothers/sisters at home. Share new lists. Read "nostalgia" poems/prose. Extend lists. Write, in poetry or autobiographical prose.

2. Double lesson reading selections of stories written in first week.

Week three (plus?)

Time poems. Reconsider (group discussion) the material from week two (1) in the light of the passage of time. Write poems.

This turned out to be a successful and very enjoyable block of work. The poetry writing reached the high standard I expected and was eventually gathered together in a typed anthology. The autobiographical writing was a delightful reminder of the pupils I knew of old, and in the work of my new group, 4/R, was the promise of good things to come. But the quality of the retellings exceeded my most optimistic prognostications. No two were quite alike: it was as though something essential of each individual's way of seeing was touched in every new telling. I will illustrate very briefly here the range of imaginative leaps which occurred as further justification of my conviction that more individuality is released during the course of a retelling than one could ever reasonably anticipate.

In my first example, the boy is truly of the countryside. It begins with his return home from gathering in the harvest, only to discover "an eerie silence in the house" and nothing of the usual sounds of movement or his mother's singing while cleaning up. After increasingly agonized searching, he finds her, face downwards on the floor of his parents' bedroom:

He ran over to her and lifted her head sharply. "Mum! Mum! Wake up!"
He tapped her cheeks lightly with his soiled hands. She did not move a
muscle. Peter felt for a pulse in his mother's neck. There was none. Her face
was white and her arms were blue. Peter clasped his hands to his face and wept
softly . . .

His father returns and he finds his son beside his mother, her head cradled on his lap:

A month later Peter's mother had been buried and forgotten about by the
village they lived in. Peter rose one bright and sunny morning, pulled aside
the curtains of his room and flung open the window. There was the smell of
cut grass, the birds singing and the sun waking up for a new day. He made his
way downstairs quietly so not to wake his dad who had not yet got over the
funeral. Into the kitchen Peter went, and opened the cupboard to get some bread.
Beside the cupboard he found a note which read, "To Peter. I am sorry, son, but
I have left. I cannot cope without your mother and I need a long time to think
things out. Goodbye."
   At first Peter did not know what to do. Could it be a joke? Was it true?
What a state this left him in! "I am going out into the world to find a place
where I can live forever," said Peter, "then I will have no more worries or
problems."
   The next morning, desperately missing his father, he set off towards the
west with some gold coins in his pocket and a knapsack of food. As he walked

along the dusty dirt track road leading from his home, Peter turned round and took a last look at the stone cottage which held so many memories for him from as far back as he could remember, when he was a little baby. He thought of the days of running around in the long grass at the back of the house trying to catch butterflies. And the time he climbed the big old fig tree for the very first time.

Goodbye. Maybe I'll return some day.

After travelling for about a day and a half, Peter came across a strange-looking old man . . .

Andrew

The next example, again from the opening of the story, draws on the fantasy of the ending of my version rather than the realism of the beginning:

Once upon a time in a small village in Italy a boy was sitting beside his mum, crying.

"What is wrong, young sir?" said a voice.

"My mother has died and I wanted her to live forever," he said, snivelling.

"Well, young sir, everyone must follow me sometime."

"What do you mean — follow me sometime?"

"I am Death. I was sent to collect your mother."

"Go away! Go away, Death! Take my mum another time!"

"I have taken your mum already. It is you I have come for."

"You are not going to get me, Death! I am going to live forever!"

"Nobody can do that, young sir. I find everybody I look for."

The boy ran out of the hut, got onto his white stallion and rode off as quick as he could . . .

Jason

Here is one with overt reflection on the events throughout:

Once upon a time in a village lived a boy named Simon. His father and mother were on their way out of the house to visit their cousins because one of them was very ill indeed. Simon thought to himself, "I wonder what it feels like to be dead."

Just at that moment his parents left, calling out goodbye at the same time. "Bye, mum. Bye, dad."

He began to wonder again. What was going to happen to him when he grows old? Why do people have to die? Suddenly something clicked in his head.

"Where there is Death there must also be Life. There must be a place somewhere on this earth where there is eternal life."

He decided that he would go and look for this place . . .

Roger

I will end this brief series of samples with one which was particularly important for me as a good augury for the coming term and year. This boy found writing difficult. So excited was he, however, at the prospect of retelling "The Land . . ." that he found himself able to produce seven sides of writing in place of the usual one. I quote Hakan here because of the clever way he manufactures a source for the boy's false hope:

> Long long time ago there lived a boy and his grandmum. The boy's grandmum was very ill and she was going to die. The boy said to his nan why do people have to die
> The old woman replied there is no reason you just do but when you do you go to a place were you live for ever. The young boy said to the old woman I am going to find that place I am sixteen now and old enouf
> So the boy got packed and started on his journey . . .

Hakan

People who have listened to my telling of this story and responded to a follow-up invitation to produce something new of their own have come up with all sorts of originality. Many have translated it into the twentieth century. At a conference I recall a version by the headmaster of a well-known public school who seemed quite annoyed by the fact that the boy loses his life on account of a good deed. In his version the boy evades the offers first of a banker wanting help in counting his money, then of an engineer who cannot see anything in life beyond his own total absorption in building bridges, and finally of a surgeon who is inundated with arms and legs to sew up in a world where there is much killing and maiming going on. The place he eventually reaches is run by someone whose motives are decidedly questionable: life in the castle (transformed to a plush country estate) is one of wealth and luxury, money, alcohol, cholesterol and many more sinful things. It is hardly surprising that from such a place comes the warning, "When you leave, do not on any account do anyone a good turn: if you do, you're sunk, mate!"

The sixteen- and seventeen-year-olds in my own school were equally inventive, and also very often eager to modernize their stories. Some waxed quite lyrical, creating old men whose tasks included counting the stars in the heavens and making a mountain out of pebbles off the beaches of the world. Younger children drew more from their repertoire of folk tales: one had a wandering soldier skirting Death and wicked monsters in a quest to find nothing more out of the ordinary than work; another dispensed with males altogether and replaced the boy of the story with a girl "with golden hair"; another's hero was Tim, who lives in a house of straw which he leaves in his bid to avoid Death, encountering first of all an old granny who sits waiting for "a giant golden bird" which is expected in a hundred years time.

There is so much of it. There is so much to tell. The preparatory notes I made look thin beside the mass that came out.

I have detailed here only what encompassed the first story of the term. The stories of Ixion, Tantalus and Sisyphus involved much more preparation, both for the storytelling and the follow-up activity which focused upon states of unending torment and the unremitting task. This gave rise to much sober talk, writing and poetry about those who have suffered in the past and those who suffer now in the hands of repressive regimes. In chapter five I mentioned the kind of texts with which I surrounded the story of Demeter — a story of motherhood, love, parting and perpetual yearning for the child who is lost. Fear of the unknown, of evil and the powers of darkness hedged about the tales of Charon and the monster dog Cerberus.

And it was all building up to the climax of our term — the story of Orpheus and Eurydice.

Eleven

STORYTELLING AND CRITICAL THINKING

"Orpheus and Eurydice" was the last and, I think, the best received of the stories I told my 4's. Listening to me telling stories had become an accepted and acceptable part of our routine. The boys and I relished it, first as a pleasant experience in itself, but also as the precursor to productive activity which left no one floundering on the sidelines. By this time many of the boys had become quite self-critical about what was happening in their work and reflective about the context of stories and the nature of narrative composition.

Even before telling the story I knew that the level of achievement of the pupils' responses would be high in both vision and language. I think I knew it even during the summer when I did the bulk of my planning. After all, we had begun with a story that reached directly into each imagination without the intrusion of any printed text, accumulated a sense of story over many weeks, and added various pieces of literature to confirm the tone of each tale.

What I did not anticipate was the amount of thinking which gathered around the edges of what I had planned and which was revealed in quantities of spontaneous talk: about the likely origins of stories; about how they might have spread from person to person, country to country, continent to continent; about why they should matter to people who made them and received them.

My next chapter will focus on the actual construction of stories and the act of creating them — an exploration that had nothing to do with traditional "lit crit" practices but had everything to do with the pupils' experience of being authors themselves and of sharing their findings as craftsmen. But let me first give an indication of the starting points of some of this thinking.

■ DISCUSSION

The Persephone/Demeter myth had given rise to discussion about the human need to find explanations for natural phenomena. Several creation myths were bandied about, as were stories from various cultures about floods as tools of revenge on the part of the god(s). There was some fierce argument at times as to what could be considered "true" religious belief and what was "mere superstition." Did god create man or man create god? The validity of the distinction was called into question.

What emerged from the writings and talk about the themes of the stories was the notion that folk stories are a way of dealing with matters of deep concern in people's lives. Discussions included references to contrasts in interpretation as the result of differences in the natures of the individual retellers. Kevin Als's "The Land . . ." cropped up a lot in this context, as its distinctiveness was obvious to everyone: after three years together the boys knew each other very well indeed.

We also noted that people are inordinately interested in their fellows, and so enjoy exploring their common and quirky ways in narrative: the ingenious mischief of Anansi, the wickedness of Ixion, the evil cunning of Sisyphus. There was more animation in the discussion of this topic because it came via told stories instead of the more formal business of "characterization" in fiction.

Through their own retellings, oral and written, the pupils discovered for themselves how stories are picked up and transmitted from one teller to another. It was easy for me, therefore, to talk about pre-Homeric orality and what became of it, or to show what Shakespeare did with Holinshed or Plutarch. And easy, too, for Harold Rosen to come into 4/C and talk about how stories change in the telling, armed with extracts from the poetry of Virgil. Though we did not get as far as the intriguing question of exactly why particular stories become universally popular, or why we are drawn by this thing called a story anyway, the boys were in no doubt about the capacity of stories to travel. They were familiar with the voyagings of Anansi, and with the fact that new stories were now cropping up which placed him in urban London. They had actually witnessed a Turkish boy insisting that the shepherd who cried "Wolf!" was a native of northern Cyprus, though we all realized he came from everywhere. What I felt was important at this stage was to illustrate the power of a good story to inspire all who create, whether the medium is language or something else.

Normally I would introduce any new work fully, explaining why I was doing what I was doing and giving the pupils an indication of what the aims and possible outcomes would be. I believe this was interpreted as "Miss going on a bit." But telling them a story was totally different — opposite, in fact. I only asked them to shove the tables to the back of the room and draw the chairs and themselves round my desk at the front. When they were settled I would launch into the tale. That was all that was necessary by way of preparation. My trust was in the story alone! However, partly because of the kind of reflection upon stories which had arisen during the preceding weeks and partly because I wanted to make a big thing of the ultimate story of the term, I decided to exploit a position of strength and set the stage for "Orpheus and Eurydice" rather more elaborately.

■ MUSIC

First I played a tape of the "Dance of the Blessed Spirits" from Gluck's *Orfeo*. Then I told them to listen to it again and write down a description of whatever pictures came into their heads. Here are some samples:

Fog is beginning to rise from the misty sea. The light on the lighthouse is shining through the mist that is thickening slowly. There are no ships to make waves on the sea, only gulls are flying over the cliffs. Soon the fog begins to clear away and the sun is peeking through.

Chi Hung

A floating lily on a stream is sailing slowly on its way. Ducks are paddling on the silvery water. Otters are bobbing up and down looking for a place to eat. Up in the sky the birds soar through the air. The trees are still, watching what is going on.

Nicholas F

People are on a boat cruise going down the River Thames at night. No waves — it's smooth and calm with an opera playing music on board the boat and everybody dancing and waltzing with the music.

Patrick

As the cool breeze swept by my warm face I said to myself — this is life; what else could a person want? Sitting at the coastline of this beach as the tide comes in it twinkles on your toes. What a lovely feeling it is.

As you are looking in the sky you see the moon going round in circles, stars moving peacefully. The scenery is so beautiful. Sometimes I want to be up there instead of this earth so peaceful it seems.

It's like flying on a carpet, care-free, believing that nothing in the world could ever happen to you, flying over mountain tops so cool, so nice.

Yawi

I think Gluck would have been quite pleased.

I then told them about the spirits of Elysium. Soon afterwards they listened to "Che farò senza Eurydice," sung first in Italian by Janet Baker, then in English, taped from a crackly old recording of Kathleen Ferrier — the very first record I had ever bought, secondhand, in the days when I didn't even have a record player! And finally they heard Alfred Deller, who several boys point-blank refused to believe was male in spite of my "going on" about altos, counter-tenors and — yes — castrati. Anyhow, they picked up bits of the melody by the end and knew what the words were about. Later on they heard Janet Baker again singing "Orpheus with his Lute."

On the Friday night before I started our Orpheus work I covered one of my display walls with postcards I had collected of people involved with music-making, lutes and lyres predominating. There were also such pictures as "Prisoners listening to music" by Kathe Kollwitz, "Famille de paysans dans un intérieur" by Le Nain, and several serene-looking individuals who (I claimed) were listening to music while being painted. I invited captions for them.

I found there was a whole string of operatic composers right up to the present day who had used the Orpheus myth: it must be the most popular of all subjects with operatic composers. I was surprised to discover that the very first opera listed in *The Oxford Companion to Music* is in fact "Euridice" by Peri, written in 1600.

■ LITERATURE

Just before I actually got round to telling the tale itself, "Miss" decided to risk a serious stint of "going on" about Milton and Shakespeare. Here is the event, recreated from memory:

> Right, you've listened to some music, done a bit of writing and had a look at a lot of pictures. The story's not far off now. The story of Orpheus. It's a great favourite, not only with people who listen to it or read it for themselves (which people have been doing for centuries) but with those whose life's work it is to create — in words, paint, stone and music.
>
> This is not just because it's a good tale but because it tells of things which have always mattered a lot to ordinary people. It's about the power of music — I mean we all like it, don't we? Music in some form or other. It can cheer us up, take our minds off our everyday troubles; and it can fit in with our moods when we feel angry or sad or romantic and so on. Sometimes it can put you into a certain mood as you saw in those bits you wrote about "The Dance of the Blessed Spirits." Anyway, this story tells of enormous wishful thinking when death carries off someone who is precious to you; that deep longing to have the loved one back again when you just can't face being alone. "What is life to me without thee?" in the song — you know. Finally it's a story of magical

deeds and fantastic places like the one where Tantalus fetched up. Everybody likes a bit of make-believe, even old grannies like you-know-who.

The story was written down first over two thousand years ago. Since then lots of writers have mentioned Orpheus in their own stories and poems. Have a look at the sheet now. I'll read the bit by a man called John Milton who lived about three hundred years ago.

In notes . . .
Untwisting all the chains that tie
The hidden soul of harmony;
That Orpheus self might heave his head
From golden slumber on a bed
Of heaped Elysian flowers, and hear
Such sounds as would have won the ear
Of Hades, to have quite set free
His half regained Eurydice.

Or bid the soul of Orpheus sing
Such notes as warbled to the string
Drew iron tears down Hades' cheek,
And made Hell grant what Love did seek.

We won't stop over those two bits now. I just wanted you to see how Orpheus is popped into other writings.

Shakespeare often put songs in his plays. Somebody would sing them on the stage. Quite often they'd be playing on a lute at the same time. Some really good songs were composed with a lute accompaniment in England about that time. Here's a song which comes in a play Shakespeare wrote, *Henry VIII*. Listen to the words — I really like them myself, I nearly know them off by heart.

Orpheus with his lute made trees,
And the mountain tops that freeze,
Bow themselves when he did sing;
To his music plants and flowers
Ever sprung; as sun and showers
There had made a lasting spring.

Everything that heard him play
Even the billows of the sea
Hung their heads and then lay by.
In sweet music is such art,
Killing care and grief of heart
Fall asleep, or hearing die.

You see. Even the waves — the billows — went calm for him. I think that's really nice, you know. I'd like to hear someone else read it. Anyone? OK, you read the first stanza and he can read the second . . . Thanks.

I've got this song on tape actually . . .   This is Janet Baker again, one of the singers you heard the other day . . .

This song has often been set to music by composers from the day Shakespeare wrote it onwards. The other day I looked through a list of operas composed up to the beginning of this century and I counted five between 1600 and 1858. In Vienna in 1762 Gluck composed his *Orfeo*. It's going to be on telly soon. It isn't very long so you could watch it and listen out for the bits you've heard . . .   Well, watch a bit of it then. You could skip *Dallas* just once.

Well, here we are in 1985, and here in our school in Tottenham stories and poems will be composed by you, based on the story of Orpheus. Perhaps some of them will be published too, and added to the long history of creative acts connected with this old myth.

Right, we'll have a little break for five minutes while you have a chat, then I'll tell you the story.

And that's just what I did.

■ ORPHEUS AND EURYDICE

Once there was a little child who amazed his family and the people living nearby in the Greek village where he was born because, at a very young age, when he began to hum and sing to himself, the sounds he made had a calming effect on all around him. The noise and bustle of the family would ease into a stillness as soon as he began to sing. When he was seven years old, his grandfather went to the marshy edges of the river which wound its way along the valley bottom and carefully chose a reed. Out of it he made a pipe for the boy. As soon as he put it to his lips, Orpheus created a melodious sound, the like of which had never been heard in those parts before. The notes wafted out through the open door into the street from the corner of the kitchen where the boy was sitting on his little wooden stool. A begger shuffling by forgot his hunger and thirst. The village bully who was hurrying past on the lookout for a new victim stopped in his tracks, listened until the boy's melody was over, and slowly wandered back the way he had come, wondering as he made his way home why his eyes had filled with tears.

As Orpheus grew older he became more and more adept in the art of making music. By the time Orpheus was 19, all the people in the village and in the locality were at the mercy of his music. By this time he had learnt to play the lute and the lyre; now he could accompany himself as he sang. The sounds of work and effort in the village would stop as soon as Orpheus began to play. The shoemaker would set aside his hammer and the huge bellows in the smithy would wheeze to a halt. The smith himself would move to the entrance of his shop and settle himself against his doorpost with a deep sigh, his big arms folded across his chest.

Sometimes Orpheus left the village and made his way into the woodlands, into the forests, to the foot of the great mountain that overlooked the village. He would wander along the edge of the river until it broadened out and joined the sea where he would gaze at the distant horizon. In the shade of a tree he would sit and make up songs about what he saw around him. Still he was not alone because the branches above his head would become heavy with the birds that had come to listen and the beasts of the forests would find their way to the source of the sound. Even the very fiercest ones would forget their bloodthirsty claws and sharp teeth and lie down to listen to the music. Indeed, some said that the tall pines of the forest bent their heads to be closer to the musician and even the frozen-topped mountain shifted a shade nearer, while the waves on the sea calmed themselves and moved noiselessly amongst the sandy pebbles on the shore.

Such was the amazing power of the music of Orpheus. Everyone loved him for they felt a richness within one who could pour forth beauty from his throat and fingertips. The girls of the village especially loved him and each thought that one day Orpheus might turn some of his attention towards her rather than exclusively to music.

A day did in fact come when he was moved by the sight of a woman, but it was not one of the village girls. He was sitting alone one sunny morning on a tree stump at the edge of a woodland playing his lute. He became aware that someone was moving towards him through the meadow. He looked up and there was a beautiful young woman who, like all living things, was drawn to Orpheus's music. He was struck by her beauty and grace. She moved with ease — it was almost as though the long grasses parted in front of her to make way for her progress towards their meeting. When she was quite close and they looked into each other's eyes it was, of course, love at first sight, and Orpheus and Eurydice did not wait long to be wed. A merry time it was for everyone in the village and for Eurydice's family and friends who arrived from their homes afar off for the celebrations on that happy day. Even the girls who had coveted Orpheus for themselves were consoled by the sight of his joy and they danced cheerfully to the music he made from it, and it was the sweetest he had ever composed. They seemed to know that this was a love that would last for all time and would be told of in stories to come by their children and their children's children. Even while they danced or stopped to laugh and chat with one another, they wondered that such love could exist in their midst.

This is where the story of these lovers should cease to be told but it was not to be so. They had been married for no more than two weeks when Eurydice, alone in the forest gathering the cool parasol mushrooms that were growing among the fallen pine needles, was suddenly startled by the appearance of an angry stranger. Instinct made her turn and run from him, scattering her harvest as she fled. She ran without looking where she placed her feet. Suddenly she felt a sharp pain in her heel which made her stumble. The pain spread fast from her foot to the whole of her body, and before falling senseless to the earth, she saw a deadly snake glide away into the ferns at the edge of the path. Within moments, Eurydice lay dead on the forest floor.

Her death brought grief to all but, of course, to none so much as Orpheus who was made desperate by the loss of the only love he had ever had and ever could have. Time ahead stretched bleak before him. He left the company of those he knew best and hid from the sun among icy crags and in the darkest, gloomiest corners of caves where he could find dismal solitude. The strings of his lyre did not stir. His songs of pleasure were but memories.

Sometimes low wailing notes welled up from his grey soul, making dirges which howled against the granite walls of the cold places where he had hidden himself away, and echoed out into the wilderness beyond. Here he would spend his days until the barren wastes merged with the gruesome dark of Hades' realm. As thoughts of the land of death slid into his mind, so too did a vision of Eurydice whose beauty would now be a match for that of Persephone herself, Queen of the Underworld.

He could not bear to think that only the hollow eyes of the dead would gaze on her sweet face. Surely there was some means of retrieving his love and bringing her back to where the sun shone and the land was green. Perhaps he, Orpheus, could fetch her back through the one power that he had, the power of music.

This thought grew and grew and carried him out of his hiding place and away to the north, to the very mouth of the tunnel that led down to the dreary realm of the Underworld. This was where he met the first of the many hazards in the way of every mortal who has dared to try to set foot in the land of the dead. There lay the huge dog Cerberus who growled with his three throats and bared his three sets of yellow fangs at anyone who stepped too close to the entrance. But Orpheus had the answer to such ferocity. He took up his lyre and gently, softly caressed its strings while humming a sweet lullaby, and approached the three-headed dog. First one head, then the next and the next lolled down over the huge paws and Cerberus slept, not knowing that a living mortal was stepping over his back and moving down into the long passageway beyond.

Orpheus made his long, dark way down until he reached the dividing line between the upper world and the lower, the oily river Styx which separated the earth from Hades. There was Charon, the boatman, waiting to receive only dead souls, each with a silver coin clutched in its hand ready to pay the ferryman. Again Orpheus played his music. Charon listened in rapture and forgot his role. When Orpheus demanded to be carried across the river of death, Charon did not turn away this living being but obeyed willingly. His only fee was, "More music! Play on, play on while I row you across!" And Orpheus played, his slow song keeping time with the soundless motion of the oars. He continued to play even as he stepped out of the boat on to the dull banks of the dead side of the river.

What a dismal region it was. What moans and cries and weepings invaded his ears. All the tormented spirits of the deep were gathered there, wailing in their perpetual pain. He took pity on these poor, suffering creatures and played soothing notes on his lyre and sang songs of sorrow shared. For them he played his sweetest music.

Their cries were lulled and all fell silent as Orpheus's music entered their ears. Sisyphus left his shameful block of stone where it had rolled and, instead of heaving it up the mountain in another everlastingly vain attempt to carry out his appointed task, he turned his tortured body towards the sound of that human voice, so beautiful in its pity, and rested his heavy head against the side of the source of his torment. Ixion's fiery wheel ceased its revolutions and became cool, or so it seemed, while Ixion himself listened to the sweet sounds, and wept for those he had harmed in his lifetime. The lean, bony hand of Tantalus gently relaxed from stretching towards the grapes that were forever poised above him and he forgot his dry throat; he thought instead of his murdered son who had risen again from that ugly fate, and Tantalus rejoiced that it was so. Every suffering heart was eased as Orpheus passed through the dank mists and on, on into the pale light of the Elysian fields where his eyes searched about frantically for a dear, familiar shape among the clouds of blessed spirits which huddled around the music-maker.

He made his way right inside the ebony palace of Hades, King of the Underworld, powerful brother of Zeus. He found himself in front of the very throne where the great angry god sat, his hair awry about his huge head and his brow creased with lines of fury at the sight of a mortal man strolling in his terrain. The god opened his mouth to make a great roar — but no sound emerged because sound came first from the throat of Orpheus and the strings of the lyre. Hades relaxed upon his throne and listened in wonder because Orpheus played as he had never played before. He played from the depths of his love and longing and he sang of the matchless beauty of Eurydice. Even Persephone, who sat languidly beside her husband, also full of longing for her mother and for the bright sunshine of the green world above, was touched with hope and felt the promise of springtime in Orpheus's music. And Orpheus played for a long time; he had to be sure that the king was truly under his spell and would grant his one wish.

When the music stopped, tears, like pebbles, were slipping down Hades' iron cheeks and, without a moment's thought as to any consequences, Hades cried out, "Oh mortal man, there is beauty beyond reward in your playing, but I will grant you anything you may desire of me!"

Orpheus wasted no time in making his request. Hades' anger began to seethe again. What a blunder he had made! What magic could have possessed him! In a moment of weakness he had made a promise and no god could go back on his word. "Yet there must be some way that I can trick this upstart fellow," he thought. "There must be some way that I can keep all my spirits to myself in my own kingdom of Tartarus."

"Oh, give this great musician his wife again," pleaded Persephone, "for remember how your love made you steal me from the world of light. Just this once, surely, you can let love pluck free but one of your subjects from this realm of darkness."

"Very well," said the king. "Leave my palace and my kingdom with your wife. Your steps must be firm and straight, for Eurydice will follow your lead. But take care, mortal, for I have one final command and you must take heed of it if your wish is to be fulfilled. On no account must you turn and look backwards towards the kingdom of the dead, not even to feast your eyes upon the one you love. Look only ahead towards the upper air, else Eurydice will be lost to you forever."

Orpheus stepped out of the palace. His heart had not been as light since the day he and Eurydice were wed. He made his way swiftly towards the grey clouds which swirled over the marshes around the River Styx. He heard nothing of the sad sounds that grew around his head from the spirits in torment and he had no words for Charon who was only too eager to ferry this mortal to the other side of the river where he belonged. In the distance was the tiny dot of light at the end of the long tunnel which was to lead him and his dear wife to united joy once more! His footsteps clattered against the hard cobbles and the echoes rang through the stone hollows. His footsteps. Only his footsteps. Orpheus held his breath and listened. Not a footstep, not a sigh, not the faintest whisper of sound came from behind his back. He walked on and on, panic mounting within him. Could it be the cruel king had tricked him into leaving with all speed, alone? The circle of light ahead expanded even as his doubts grew larger with each step he took.

"Eurydice! Eurydice! Are you there?" he called in anguish. There was no reply. Nothing. Empty silence. He could see the dark shape of Cerberus across the mouth of the tunnel and white clouds above him. He could see, now quite clearly, the three heads, the bristling hairs over each sleeping eye. Beyond he could see the hanging boughs of a willow tree swaying gently in the fresh breeze that touched his cheek. "Eurydice!" he cried. "Answer me now!"

A terrible madness engulfed Orpheus and, on the very brink of light, he turned his head to look over his shoulder.

In that instant, a mighty clap of thunder rolled over the pools where Tantalus sorrowed. Eurydice, her arms outstretched towards her only love, was sinking away from him into endless night, dissolving out of sight like smoke into thin air, leaving Orpheus to grasp vainly at shadows.

It is said that Orpheus never ceased to mourn his love and, one day, the women thereabouts who felt themselves despised fell upon him and tore him to pieces. His severed head — or so the story goes — was cast into the river and, as the currents bore it away, his icy tongue sang out one word, "Eurydice!" and then was heard no more.

Twelve

THE POWER OF AUTHORS

My pupils' performances as authors — members of a long line of interpreters of the Orpheus and Eurydice story — met all my expectations. First it might be appropriate to look at a complete retelling, if only to demonstrate that all the preparatory work I described was worthwhile! It was written by Che, aged fourteen.

■ CHE'S STORY

From the day that Orpheus could speak he could sing. At first there were only gurgles but as he got older so the melodies came. These were not just familiar tunes; at first he copied any song but then he started to compose.

And when he sang and played his lyre he rivalled the birds in the trees — once or twice he even heard the birds copy him. He would sit in the forest and play. Wild beasts of every size and shape would listen to the lullaby that Orpheus would compose on the spot. Baby antelope would cuddle together close to the bear's fur coat on a cold night and on a warm summer's day humming birds would fly about the lion's mane, causing the king of the beasts to roll over playfully. This mysterious power of music would tame wild beasts and stop the wind from chasing its tail among the trees and make him pause before carrying the sweet music to the rest of the land, as if to say "Look what I picked up on my travels." The trees stopped their endless secret whispers and stood in silence. Even Hades would be moved, so Orpheus's father said.

Yes, Hades. Surely he must understand my love for my lost Eurydice. Maybe I can lull him — or his wife — into a state of compassion. No! My Eurydice is gone. It is no use trying to get her back; no one cheats death. But in Orpheus's mind another voice said, no one has the weapon you have got.

Orpheus shivered in the wet cave and went into an uneasy sleep with his back against the wall — something firm to hold on to, to keep his mind from slipping away. When Orpheus woke up he felt something slither away from his leg. He looked down, and with a cry of rage he grabbed the snake by its neck and its body curled round his arm. "Serpent, your kind thought it could separate my wife Eurydice and me forever but I shall have the final victory. I shall reclaim my love straight from the silent depth of Tartarus. I shall plead with Hades himself for the release of Eurydice. He threw the writhing body out of the cave and set off with a determined stride towards the entrance of Hades.

He came to a large marble arch, big enough for gods, centaurs, giants, any who might need to enter the gate of Tartarus. As he stepped inside into the narrow tunnel he was shocked out of a daydream, a trance, in which he lived again a fortnight's married love which was to be spoilt on just such a day as this. It was Cerberus who shocked him for the dog was chained to the wall but the chain let Cerberus reach the other side of the passage. To get past would mean stepping over Cerberus's three heads.

Orpheus knew the time had come to test his music. He started to play, and the middle head began to remember when it was part of a real dog and not a monster, when it had a real human master and was not ruled by an unfeeling god. He lay himself down, and remembered barking happily, not growling in an uncontrolled fury. Cerberus fell asleep and Orpheus stepped into the underworld.

At the end of the tunnel he came to a river bank where there was a murky black river with a grey mist a few centimetres above its surface which swirled about in an unfelt wind. Orpheus was pondering over how to get across when out of the darkness came a voice.

"Who wishes to cross the River Styx?"

"Tis I, Orpheus."

"You have the fare?"

"Yes!" Orpheus felt bitterly cold. "Hurry or I'll freeze."

A splashing sound came out of the mist and a boat appeared with an oarsman completely covered in cloth who said, "I, Charon, immortal oarsman of the River Styx, brought down from the land of the living by Hades on the creation day of this realm, Tartarus, have seen and heard many things but I have never heard of a dead man speak of the cold."

Orpheus gasped.

"Mortal, what are you doing alive in Hades and what happened to Cerberus?"

Orpheus did not want to answer. A feeling of dreadful horror came over him. He had caught a glimpse under the cloak. Charon was a skeleton hung with bits of burnt flesh. Orpheus swallowed his fear and said, "What do the dead know of love? When my love was at my side we stayed together for less than two weeks. I want more. She was bitten by a serpent in the grass and died in another's arms. I have come for Eurydice."

Orpheus played his lyre softly and the underworld was quiet, straining to hear his voice and lyre. Then he stopped and from all around in chorus the inhabitants of Hell screamed for Orpheus to play on. Charon promised that if Orpheus would play on he would ferry him across. Orpheus played and sang in the light and heat of a burning wheel that followed behind. The souls in Hades were resting. They were flooded with feelings from the past. Orpheus had brought them close to the life they would never again see.

In the middle of all this chaos were two thrones. On one sat a pretty young maiden; on the other a big, brawny god with grey eyes, cold and calculating. Orpheus turned his gaze away from Hades and started to play to his wife, Persephone. He was giving Hades no chance to vent his anger on him but in Hades' eyes he saw the fires of hate dim so he paused.

"Play on, mortal. You are not the first to enter the underworld but your music has got you farthest. With your tunes you can change the moods of the gods and I grant your any wish."

When Orpheus had finished playing he asked for what he wanted and Hades stormed and raged. Then he decided. "Orpheus, your wish is granted but Eurydice will walk behind you and if you look back you shall lose her forever."

Orpheus left, calling, "Eurydice, Eurydice! Come closer. I cannot hear you!"

He was scared. Had Hades deceived him? She wasn't on the boat. He could hear nothing in the empty tunnel. As he approached Cerberus he could control himself no longer. He turned.

"Orpheus!" her voice faded. "What have you done?"

■ GROWING CRAFTSMANSHIP

I also want to give in this chapter an indication of the way the pupils had matured as technicians. Over the term I had come to enjoy the ease and evident spontaneity with which the boys got down to their retellings. As time went on, their analysis of the composing process became similarly spontaneous while they listened to and talked about each other's versions. My version, too, was involved in these discussions. It would be referred to frequently to highlight new approaches, noticeably different language usage or obvious changes and extensions. And I would find myself saying things like: "Oh, that's quite different from what I said" or "I prefer your wording of that episode" or "I would never have thought of doing it like that." I am utterly persuaded that the effect of all this was to make them more conscious of the power of the author than any other type of activity in previous English lessons ever had — the infinity of choices available to creators and the potential to be absolute master of the artifact.

I remember exploring with them how they set about their task, specifically how they decided at what point they would begin. During this discussion I "went on" at some length about my own agonizing over how I should begin the story of Persephone. The effect was to put the openings of stories into sharp focus and from that point there was suddenly a much wider — and more accomplished — range of story openings from the boys. It does not take a very great leap of the imagination to realize how this advance would permeate whole pupil texts.

Easily, informally, we had shared the experience of looking objectively at finished products. By the time they came to write their own versions of Orpheus, many of the boys had learned to take delight in consciously shaping ideas and crafting language to their own purposes. The classroom had become a sort of writers' workshop, and the people in it conscious of their own authorship.

The samples below highlight the pupils' progression from writing "instinctively" to writing as craftsmen, especially with reference to the way they chose to begin their versions. Some, of course, began "at the beginning," with Orpheus's childhood or youth as a budding musician — much in the way that I did in my version. But many did not, evidently engaging in a process of selection not dissimilar to the one I described in chapter five. Here are some illustrations:

"Look at him! He's going to the woods again," shout the women of the village. They point to a young man holding a lute. This was Orpheus, the great lute player.

Michael P

Eurydice was walking through the woods with one of the village girls, quite unaware of the danger which lurked nearby in the shape of a deadly venemous serpent. As Eurydice got closer the serpent came from beneath its bush and struck with deadly accuracy upon her foot.

Chris N

"Come on, Orpheus, do I not tempt you? Am I not prettier than the others?" She closes in on Orpheus and wraps herself around him.

"I have no time for your pretty fancies. Are you interested in me or just in proving yourself to the other spinsters in the village?"

The girl backed away like a child who didn't get the toy it wanted.

John

"Eurydice! Eurydice!" his voice echoes, rolling down the tunnel.

Hakan

Orpheus, with one hand holding the lyre that he always cared for and loved like his own brother, set off upon the dangerous journey to Hades, the journey that could lead him to death and torment. But that did not stop him. For the love of Eurydice he carries on; even now he has reached the foot of the mountain where in front of him is the entrance to the underworld from which he might never return. Then inside the cave loud, echoing footsteps blast out, slowly a head appears, then two, then three. It is Cerberus, the three-headed dog.

Chi Hung

As the tragedy of Eurydice was bestowed on him, Orpheus was thrown into indescribable grief because, you see, he had never had any time for women.

From the time he was knee high his grandmother had bought him a lyre and that was his life until he met Eurydice. He had fallen in love with her on first sight and now he had lost her.

Errol

The bells rang all through the town where Orpheus was marrying his lovely new wife Eurydice. Not many marriages were perfect in Greece at this age of time but so many people believed that these two would make the perfect couple.

Yawi

Orpheus fell to the ground on hearing the news. Tears filled his eyes as he started to cry in grief, for his own Eurydice had been bitten by a serpent and had died immediately on the same spot.

Kevin S

All those openings presaged versions which, though enormously different from one another, preserved the "facts" and the tone of the version the writers had heard from me. Here are some which moved substantially away from it in one respect or another:

"Master, wake up!"
"Shut up, slave!"
Rossi, the slave of the musician, and his master went down to breakfast. Orpheus would ask Rossi where they were going to play and the reply was "the forest" or "the river" or "shut up." Ten minutes later Orpheus began to put his equipment on. Yes, Orpheus was what we now call a one-man band. There was only one thing wrong: his music was terrible, so bad he was begged to stop.
"OK, Rossi, let's go."
Rossi was a clever bastard. He took half a pound of cheese with him to block his ears.

Michael M

Orpheus, as far as anyone could remember, had always had a beautiful voice. Some say he was given the gift by Calliope. Rumour has it that she came to Orpheus' parents just before they were born and told them that their son was to be called Orpheus and that he would be renouned for his voice and his music.

Gary

Gary goes on to describe how the nineteen-year-old Orpheus, in mystical fashion reminiscent of Excalibur appearing from the lake, receives a silver lyre from the goddess herself.

There was a man named Orpheus. He was famous for his human beat box. He lived in a little town called Liverpool.

Patrick

Orpheus and Eurydice had been married for some months now but Eurydice had changed from a loving and caring wife to a horrible nagging one. Orpheus still cared for her just as he used to do but Eurydice just didn't. After a few years she got tired of Orpheus's music and she couldn't stand him singing.

Chris T

The last one begins at the end. Or does it? Perhaps it will surprise you as it did me:

As Orpheus walked up the narrow passage which leads to our world he was worried. Had the evil king tricked him? This worried him a lot but nevertheless he did not turn to look back for he and Hades had made an agreement before they left; Eurydice must not go beside him but she may follow after him. On his way Orpheus must not look back before they went out into the sunlight or Eurydice would have to stay in the underworld for ever. Orpheus had no choice but to obey.

Just before he stepped into the sun shine he could not control his fear of leaving the underworld without her, unable to come back again. He turned, and saw Eurydice, helplessly disappearing into the darkness.

From that day onwards Orpheus was seen no more. Some rumours say he was torn to bits by the women while some say he was bitten to death by Cerberus, the three headed dog and some even say that he went back into the underworld again and never returned. But whatever is the truth only god will know.

"Why did Orpheus go into the underworld? How come Eurydice was in the underworld?" asked a boy who had just joined the group of children who sat around the storyteller and listened to him telling the story of Orpheus and Eurydice.

"Why are you so late?" asked a girl in the group.

"Yes, we have just finished the story," said another.

"Never mind," said the storyteller, "I will tell it once again for you. OK?"

Once upon a time, in a village was a boy called Orpheus. From the day of his birth he loved music . . .

Kin Tai

I have a method of assessing my own writing as it disappears into my word processor. I print out a hard copy as soon as I have finished three or four pages, and then have a sensible read. This is simply because I don't dare allow whole chapters of my painfully executed typing to lurk in the dark infernal regions, perhaps to disappear forever within the Tartarus of the machine. I am so afraid of it — its featureless, expressionless face, its independent mutterings and buzzing soliloquies, its infinite unknown quantity of unused power which I still suspect is out to get me. We have a total of three different manuals, plus the several pages it told us to print off from its "Teach yourself Locoscript" disk, which cheatingly amounts to a fourth. I can't understand any of them. I should have made backup disks while going along, but early on I was too scared of blowing the whole thing up in the attempt, and the more I put in, the more I was afraid I'd lose what I'd got altogether by making some small error in the transfer process, thus calling forth perhaps a Tantalus-sized punishment for a minor sin. In half a century of having to learn new things, nothing so much as the learning of word processing has sent me into a state of hysteria. Halfway through my second lesson at evening class, surrounded by silently self-contained secretaries beavering away with all their fingers, apparently unperturbed by the mindless array of black-magic instructions preceding their union with the familiar keyboard, I suddenly found myself fighting to contain a fiendish howl of anguish before hurtling myself out of the room and beyond, screaming, into the night.

Maybe that's how Lenny felt when he faced the prospect of writing a book review. Maybe it was a taste of what many pupils feel, particularly inner-city ones, when locked in by the uncrackable demands of an alien classroom. Some sit through it, numbly, miserably still, as I did, unable to begin to explain to the tutor that it was not *something*, but *everything*, which was beyond me.

Such feelings are the antithesis of what my pupils felt, all of them, when they got down to writing their versions of the Orpheus myth. They were so clever! The most able produced highly accomplished stories, some of enormous length. The others produced very entertaining, attractive work and even the "weakest" wrote very competently with here a word, there a phrase, a sentence or even a paragraph of excellence.

I shall select from the mass a few items to show something of the fine detail, the purple passages, the originality, the mastery of dialogue, quoting from the entire ability range:

Cerberus was standing there with saliva dripping from its mouths . . .
The temptation was too much. He looked round to see Eurydice disappear before his eyes. He called to her, but nothing. Cerberus stepped out of the shadows, pounced on Orpheus and ripped him apart. Orpheus's head rolled out of the cave, moaning for Eurydice.

Nicholas F

The only joy he used to get was when he went into the fields and played his lyre. Only then did he feel all his burdens loosened from his back.

Chris T

So Orpheus set off, not knowing where but getting there anyhow. Before long he found himself at a small opening between two boulders with a slab on top to make a sheltered doorway, dark and uninviting. One step under the slab and four yellow evil eyes blinked on and out poked two black heads. Orpheus had encountered Cerberus.

"Go away, mortal!" it snarled.

Orpheus moved forward. At this the two headed dog emerged to show Orpheus the size of body possessed by the two heads, a massive black monster of a dog, powerful limbs supporting its lithe body. Menacingly it moved forward but instead of Orpheus retreating he stood stock still and raised his lyre. He played music and sang about the stars and the moon and all the heavens. This made Cerberus pause for it had been a long time since he could enjoy such beautiful songs. He lay down on the grey floor, head on his front paws, and dozed off while the music got sweeter and gentler. Before long Cerberus had fallen into a sleep and could dream again about those long nights beside the fire with a big leg of meat in front of him or of all those hunting trips with his former master.

Gary

Sitting silently upon the river was a small boat and within the boat was a hooded figure. Orpheus walked boldly up and asked the boatman to take him across. Then slowly from one of the long sleeves came a lean hand, but this was no ordinary hand. This was the hand of a skeleton. A low voice said, "You must pay me."

Hades himself sat on his mighty throne, laughing. When he set eyes on Orpheus his happiness changed to sheer anger. "What," he boomed, "is this, a mere mortal entering the realm of Hades? Be gone, or you will surely die!"

Chris N

Charon said, "Have you got the silver coin?" and Orpheus said no so Charon said "I cannot take you." So Orpheus started playing the music and then he stopped.

Charon said, "Don't stop. Keep on playing. I'll give you anything."

Razwan

Orpheus was now in Elysium where he stood before Hades.

"Mortal, you are in this far. What have you to say?"

"I come for my Eurydice"

Hades red eyes centred on Orpheus. "You passed Cerberus and Charon just for Eurydice?" His voice echoed around Orpheus as if to break him.

Kevin A

Charon rowed Orpheus across the River Styx. Orpheus got out of the boat and moved out into the darkness. He then heard noises of pain and punishment and all the tortures of this world.

Roger

I am Orpheus, living mortal of music. One afternoon Eurydice and I were in the fields where the bluebells grow and the wild roses reach to the sky and the red poppies danced. I was playing my lyre to Eurydice. Above the sky was blue like her eyes and her lips are like a poppy rosy red and her hair is golden like the sun.

Nicky B

Orpheus was the sort of music lover who loved his music more than the village girls. One day he saw a beautiful girl called Eurydice.

Naresh

"Who are you, mortal, to charm your way past Cerberus the serpent who sees all and to come hippety hoppity into Hades? But you forget, immortal gods see all." As Charon said these words Orpheus brought his lyre up high and began to play hard, then softly after then softer. Charon's face turned from anger to a happy smirk. As Orpheus saw the change he cut the music instantly.
"No, mortal, don't stop, mortal. More, more!"
"Take me across the river of death for I have no money only sorrow and delightful music."

Errol

Attach all these to Che's, and to the story-starters quoted earlier, and it adds up very sweetly.

Thirteen

REFLECTIONS ON AUTHORSHIP

In July 1985, I had come across a book by Lotte Moos which contained a story titled "Orpheus and the Bear," and when my plan for the term's work on narrative began to take shape in my head a month later, I had no doubts about including it. Its place, however, would have to come after the 4's had both heard my more conventional version of the Orpheus myth and themselves composed versions of their own. Then, and only then, would we read together this new interpretation. Maybe, with a bit of luck, this Lotte Moos could be tracked down and persuaded to come to the school and talk about it herself, and about Hackney Writer's Workshop, to which she evidently belonged.

■ ORPHEUS AND THE BEAR

When Orpheus the musician played the lyre — or so the story goes — wild beasts would come out of the forest to listen to him. True, some, perhaps because they couldn't bear such sad music, slunk away; some yawned a little, but stayed, closing their eyes; but the ones with the hardest hearts, hearts so hard they hurt deep in their chests, would sink to the ground and moan.

But the story says nothing about the bear, a big and cruel animal, who wouldn't be won over.

"Listen, my friend," the bear said, "this isn't very gay. I want to dance. We animals come here, some from a long way off, to hear music, not to roll on the ground and snivel. Why don't you forget about your fiancé. Life ought to be jolly. Now you just let me tell you how to play!"

Orpheus handed him the lyre but the bear who, clever though he was, couldn't have told a lyre from a penny-whistle, would have none of it: "Oh no," he said, "you won't get out of it this way. You're the musician, you've got the feelings, that's what you're here for. So, why not oblige your fellow-creatures and play the way I tell you? Go on!"

Orpheus took the lyre back and tried, but now the notes came out in a plangent, discordant jangle so that the animals raised their heads and grew restless. "You taking the mickey?" the bear cried. "You're upsetting everybody. Next thing we know these lions here will have torn you to bits. And you needn't think I'll stick my nice brown neck out for you. Let's have some polkas and military two-steps, the kind of thing we all like."

And Orpheus tried hard but the harder he tried, the shriller the music got and the polkas and mazurkas and military two-steps turned round and round in crazy circles, scraping and screeching — like dirges where everybody has to beat his chest and howl.

"Stop this!" the bear cried, "I said, I want to dance, not to turn somersaults like a tom-cat with a hornet in its arse. Nor do I want these nice brown ears of mine to fall off, with having to listen to this caterwauling. But I can see, I'll have to teach you a lesson." And he raised his powerful paws.

But the other animals, not wanting to be witnesses, slank off and hid in the forest.

Orpheus sank to his knees, crying: "I've tried. You saw how hard I tried to please you. But I can't help it if, all the time, all the time, I keep thinking of . . ." but he couldn't get himself to pronounce Euridice's gentle name, alone with that awful bear standing over him — everybody else having left.

"Fuck Euridice," cried the bear, "there's plenty more where she comes from. Anyhow, some people deserve all they get" and, pretending to hit a fly on his neck, he kept looking over his shoulder, winking with his awful little brown eye.

Then Orpheus stood up and played and the bear danced. And Orpheus went on playing on and on and on, and now the bear had to go on dancing. On and on they went, Orpheus strumming the strings of the lyre, wilder and wilder, harsher and harsher, polkas and mazurkas and military two-steps, and the animals who had fled to the forest heard, and their hair stood on end and the lion rent the lamb, and the goose had its neck bitten right through by the fox, and the wolf dug out the innards of the donkey, and the horses, manes streaming, stampeded, screaming, for everywhere in the forest, there was blood.

And still Orpheus went on playing and the bear, who at first had waved his paws at Orpheus, shouting as if he were drunk: "Louder! Louder!" began to puff, his feet tripped and fumbled and he looked at Orpheus as if he really would have liked him to stop, and then he started stumbling and fell, again and again, he stumbled and, each time, took a little longer about getting up again. But up he had to get, to go on dancing, plopping his feet any old place, to the crazy tunes of the lyre, till his throat was gasping for breath and his eyes were beseeching Orpheus to stop — for there was no more breath left in him to beseech Orpheus in any other way.

And that was how Orpheus, the musician, wove an untearable net out of polkas, mazurkas, cha-chas and military two-steps and tied the bear up in it.

Then the beasts, coming out of the forest, saw that Orpheus' hair had gone grey, his fingers swollen as big as roots and all that was left of him was just a scarecrow. And they came and licked the scarecrow's hands and face, kind of hoping he'd play again. But he was too far gone to feel it.

■ RESPONSES

There is no definitive interpretation of Lotte's tale. No set of pupils' notes could justifiably be compiled for regurgitation upon an examination answer sheet. This "retelling" is so replete with symbols that a reading of it inevitably involves wrestling with multiple layers of meaning, meanings which are not necessarily encapsulated in the text but which may spring out of the fertile soil of the reader's responses. Such responses will be conditioned by each reader's personal experience of the story of living.

My own first response was powerfully charged with memories of the bleakest moments from my own past when I would turn to music for comfort, finding all other sources of distraction useless. However, it seemed likely that the author's message was primarily a political one about the effect of brutal power upon those who speak with the tongues of angels. I found myself lingering more and more upon the role of the bystanders, the animals, who, having been swayed from one extreme to the other, finally creep back for the balm which can be provided only by the message-making of an Orpheus. My years of listening to young people had also indicated that, in the final answer, people are won over by the spirit of Friday's child in the rhyme — the one who was "loving and giving" — rather than destructive forces, whether from without or within themselves.

This story, which I read to the group, made a strong impact. I can always tell if something has gone down well before anyone even opens his mouth. It was clear from the minimal comments just before I hurried the boys into small groups to discuss the story amongst themselves that feelings were mixed. Some were impressed and excited; others were outraged by what seemed to them a sacrilegious lowering of the tone of the original. Oddly — or perhaps not — the toughest characters among the 4's and 5's I read the story to took the deepest offence! All were absorbed by it and got into their discussions with no fuss.

I wanted the group talk to be as free as possible but I did direct to the extent that I asked them to try to establish what the story was getting at — what the Bear represented, what the role of the animals might be, etc. I was really very interested to know what they thought and to that end I actually taped the whole-class discussions which took place when the small groups had had their fill. Though I have had more satisfying exchanges about this story with adult friends, I think the pupils showed a sound feel for it.

Here is an extract from the discussion that went on when 4/C reported back from their small group talk:

Errol: We thought that the bear, like, he came from Hades and he's supposed to be wicked, he's supposed to torment Orpheus.

Che: I thought it was, like, another part of Orpheus himself. It could have been out of his mind, like, telling him to forget Eurydice and then he's trying to play something different and he can't.

Kevin A: The bear was trying to overpower Orpheus but when Orpheus realized that he just played so much that the bear had to stop.

Earl: I think that when the animals get together to overpower Orpheus they are all friends and everything and they don't think "Ah, I like eating that thing [*another creature*] and when the bear made Orpheus change his music they all turned evil and against each other.

Me: What is it about the change in the music that makes them like that?

Jason: The bear wanted Orpheus to play the march like thing, the war march, so it seemed like a war march.

Errol: When they started to eat the other animals it was sort of like war.

Me: But the military two-step was just one kind of dance. What do you think it was in general about the music?

Ernest: The bear, like, he had a sort of thing over Orpheus . . .

Me: A power over him?

Ernest: Yes, that made him play a different sort of music and when he wanted him to play the bad music like the march, Orpheus couldn't control himself . . . sort of like a power came over him.

Che: And when they came out of the jungle after he'd been playing it was like as if he'd had torture and all his hair had gone grey and his fingers were solid.

Me: What exactly was his torture, then?

Pupils: Playing bad music.

I wish now that I had set up each group with its own tape recorder. I have a strong feeling that the talk in the small groups was a good deal more effective. It is often a frustrating business to move around the groups picking up all sorts of interesting bits and pieces which don't seem to emerge during the plenary "feedback" session later on. During that work I have a distinct recollection of hearing someone say, "Orpheus couldn't ever win against someone like the bear — he's a right old tyrant," and someone else, "The bear kills himself by doing his own evil." These remarks come just that shade nearer to the political and moral implications of Lotte's story.

I read the story to four other classes within the space of two weeks — the other 4, two 5's and a 6 — and taped each whole-group discussion. An extraordinary richness of responses emerged.

They saw the Bear variously as a symbol of evil or death or annihilation; of power which is jealous of popularity perceived elsewhere. ("Orpheus attracts the animals but the Bear doesn't" and "The Bear likes to show that he's the top person among the animals.") Several boys referred to him as the embodiment of the desire to interfere with and deface whatever moves the human spirit to tenderness.

Some pupils reacted quite lyrically to this Orpheus and the power of his music which, when falling upon the ears and souls of the animals, "takes their breath away"; "makes them feel sad but calm." It was "music which tells of peace and love"; Orpheus "puts his heart into his music." They saw this retelling as a representation of a duel — "love versus evil"; "good against bad"; "music power"; "love power versus physical force."

Inevitably there was plenty of disagreement as to who is defeated in this tale — Orpheus, said most, because "he gets old." "He shrivels up because he has to play rubbish music"; "boogy music"; "Heavy Metal." One boy vehemently argued that Orpheus had lost most because "he can't play his own music anymore. Playing the Bear's music destroys Orpheus's soul." Others, on the other hand, stressed that eventually Orpheus took control of the Bear. No one saw any winners, needless to say, but most agreed that the animals prove to be the inheritors of the sensitivity enshrined in Orpheus's music because they return to lick his hand, "as if to say 'Come and play sweet music.' " Another pupil observed, "They are soft animals now."

Discussion turned at some point in each class to the style of Lotte's story which was referred to by several as "modern." One pupil (who was himself an expert in turning the air blue!) waxed long and irately about what he called the "cockneyization" of the language, which he considered cheapening.

In all this talk the pupils' own language flowed freely. There was none of the inhibition that comes from a request for a book review or from the traditional demand for a consideration of plot, characterization, style, etc. in a formal essay. All our interchanges, and those of subsequent discussions concerning the composition of this story in particular and stories in general, were inextricably bound up with the living story of their own growing authorship and — as I shall now relate — the exciting story of our encounter with the author of "Orpheus and the Bear" herself.

■ MEETING THE AUTHOR

I sent a transcript of all the tapes to Lotte Moos herself as an introduction to the kind of pupils she would meet when she made her visit. With hindsight I fear I intruded and directed too much. Yet there is enough in the extracts above to show that the boys responded intelligently to what was read to them and were aware of the ambiguities of the outcome of the confrontation between Orpheus and the bear.

Meeting Lotte Moos brought to mind far-off memories of my classroom in Clydach when wonderful questions hung around. What experiences, what feelings, what wealth of reflections lie hidden behind a mere face? Here was a tiny, elderly, quizzically smiling lady who, it was said, had lived through epic adventures in her time. Here she was in the flesh, venturing again to be a stranger among the strangers of my classroom. 4/C, I think, felt something of the same sense of wonder and it made them close up behind their own faces. I think they were aware of the power within this gentle person, our author for that one lesson, the last lesson of the week. It subdued them and made them shy so that — to add to my spilling cup of worries over the well-being of a visitor to the classroom — I feared they would seem to her unresponsive. Inside their outsides, however, I knew the opposite was the case, and I determined, somehow, to prove as much to her.

She let me have the notes she made for that lesson, so with their aid I can give a clear idea of what the author of "Orpheus and the Bear" had to say to 4/C.

First she said she was surprised by what the boys had said, as recorded in the transcript I had sent her. She said she was not a professional writer. She wrote, she said, mainly at night "in the dark!" to and for herself, but "the writer isn't always the best judge, neither before nor after, of what has been written, what has been let loose." She added that when writing a story she could never be quite sure how it would finish until she reached the end.

From this point Lotte talked a good deal about the differences between a myth and a fable. Fable she illustrated with reference to two stories from Aesop, "The Wolf and the Lamb" and the fable of the mute who, wrongfully accused of stealing his master's fish, was able to reveal the guilty party by indicating that all the suspects should drink a jug of salty water: the thief vomitted up the stolen fish (not a pretty tale!). A fable is "a demonstration, an application," whereas a myth is open to interpretation, to what the reader brings to it. "It forms part of you . . . It enriches you when it forms part of you."

Thinking of this now, I am reminded of a recent visit I made to a synagogue to see what a service there would be like. The text was a difficult one from Leviticus, and the Rabbi took a little time out of the Hebrew to talk about some of the different interpretations which had been put upon it by various rabbinical commentators. He seemed to be saying that where the text of the Torah is not explicit, and therefore open to interpretation, its value is not so much in its definitive — though hidden — truth but in its capacity to elicit wisdom in the reader as interpreter. It seems to me, from hearing and reading the retellings of stories I have told, that every "felt" retelling brings forth its own wisdom, its own truth.

Then Lotte focused upon the Orpheus myth itself. Like summer, she said, like life, like the psalmist's dream of the wolf that "shall dwell with the lamb," Eurydice is what has been lost or what can only come in a distant and mythical future. The animals in her story are tied to their present, their hunger, and the author cannot even let them witness the bear's doings. The bear represents power, but also the fact that power is limited by the pragmatic, separated from the feelings: "feeling is a special job." His coarse language is used "to degrade the dream — like using a crucifix as a dartboard." It reduces the love between Orpheus and Eurydice to mechanical sex: "Power fears what isn't mechanical. Only the mechanical can be controlled." Lotte went on to assert the unquestionability of Orpheus's state of being — something which is without a judgement, without irrelevant rationalization. But the bear, in his emptiness of heart, makes his judgement with his reference to those who "deserve all they get." "This is politics," Lotte added, "rubbing salt in each other's weaknesses: 'you too!'" How right that is!

"Orpheus mourns. Mourning is one kind of remembering. Power does not want us to mourn or remember." And we were all reminded of the current news bulletins telling of the funerals of assassinated black victims of the South African bear, funerals which were soon to be diminished and banned altogether. "Power cannot tolerate even the music that touches the heart, that mourns, that is not 'rubbish music.'"

Finally Lotte talked about the ending of her story, where the bear destroys Orpheus by frightening him into making a music which is alien to his own heart, at the end of which he is "too far gone to feel it" — a scarecrow. And the animals have fallen back upon themselves, their hunger, their self-destruction. But power cannot know what its final effect will be: "In the end, power will be trapped by what it has let loose." Her emphasis was upon the destruction of Orpheus, and yet she conceded that the pupils could be right: "Maybe the animals are the winners. Because if Orpheus recovers . . . Myth is circular, it starts again."

Yes, indeed. Nothing really kills Orpheus, any more than the king who promises never to chop anyone's head off can eliminate the singing spirit of humankind. So many stories, much less heroic ones, tell of indomitable human energy in pursuing the impossible goal which sits at the foot of the rainbow, at the end of the world or in the land where there are no endings. The last words of another composition by Lotte Moos, *Orpheus in the Stadium*, which records how Pinochet's men smashed the wrists of the musician under a hot Chilean sun, are these: "But even that was not the end."

■ THOUGHTS BEHIND CLOSED FACES

All this, and 4/C were subdued. She was not to know that at the end of the week they would not normally drink in every word, as they had done for her; she could not know that even the most cynical member of the group was to say to me after she had left, "She was good, that Lotte Moos, she was a good old lady." Had she been disconcerted or hurt by their silence? She said not. But to be on the safe side I followed up the lesson by collecting their reactions in written form and sending them off to her. It was quite a weighty document which included some amazing versions of the Aesop's fables she had told.

Here is just the opening of Gary's story of the mute:

Kneeling on his fluffy carpet was the great sage of Eastern Persia, pruning all those odd bits of fluff, snipping here and pricking there. All day he did this until hunger overtook his obsession. All he eats is fish (of no particular variety) and a goblet of wine and then it's straight back to his carpets.

One day the sage got hungry prematurely and so he asked his servant to get his fish and wine for him. The servant promptly vanished into the kitchen, not wishing to anger his master. When he got there, on the table was the goblet of wine and the plate for the fish but there was no fish . . .

I wanted to demonstrate to her that even a fable could be remoulded, could "form a part of you . . . enrich you."

I will end this section with some extracts from 4/C's reflections both upon the author's words and upon writing. Here is evidence that, behind closed faces, thoughts were whirring.

MOURNING IS IMPORTANT.

I think mourning is important. When a person dies and that person is very close to you I think it is essential to mourn to show your sadness and respect. According to different people's religions different ceremonies will take place e.g., in Mauritius if a close friend or relation dies and that person is very close to you then to show your respect you mustn't eat meat for a few days and you mustn't go to any parties or things like that for a few weeks. I think this is right and extremely necessary.

When my grandfather was over here on holiday we talked and began to know each other very well, then one day to my great horror he died in my house at about 9:45 p.m.! The very same day my mother phoned all our close and distant family and told them of the bad news. That night all of our relatives came to our house to show their sadness and respect. My relations stayed up until the morning, not having a wink of sleep.

I myself felt very depressed at seeing everyone mourning.

                                                            Kevin S

I think that mourning is a way of expressing one's feelings, a way of remembering a person who is lost. It is important because we are all human beings, we all have feelings which we have to express to one another. We cannot just forget what we have lost and look forward to the future. When Orpheus had lost Eurydice he mourned a lot because the feeling of loss was too strong to be overcome quickly. The same thing happens again in the funerals in South Africa. During those funerals people mourn a lot and that reminds them of the people who have died during the unrest.

Kin Tai

With mourning you can reach a certain stage and it gets no better; you have walked that road before so there is no need to go on mourning; if you don't let it out you may build up hate for other people and all you want is to be with the one who is dead and you may very well try. If you bottle up your grief any person who tries to help you share your grief you will want to have no part of it which can hurt their feelings.

Errol

I disagree with this because I can't understand why it is a necessary part of dying, to mourn. Although everyone's different they have to express their feelings in some way — I can't deny them that — but those who die most certainly would like them to remember the happy times not the sad.

Gary

THE HEART CANNOT BE CONTROLLED.

Say you are a pupil and the teacher is shouting at you for something you didn't do you would want to say what was in your heart and you would be longing to say it but the teacher says "shut up." He or she is stopping you speaking your mind but nobody can really stop those feelings.

Nicky B

As Lotte Moos said (I agree), anything which is not mechanical cannot be controlled. However hard the oppressive power tries our hearts cannot be controlled and our fear won't disappear but it will grow.

Many people in the past or in the present who are imprisoned for their belief will not change their mind about what they believe. Like Stalin, Trotsky or Lenin and other Bolshevik leaders in Russia before the first world war. They had all been sent to prison or exile for what they believed. But oppressive power could not control their hearts, their feeling and their belief and they never gave up their Marxist belief but instead they planned their revolution and continued developing their ideas.

Kin Tai

Pacemakers can control the heart in the body so why can't the [metaphorical] heart be controlled as well? People can be forced to do things against their will. People can also be brainwashed. Power is something that cannot be defeated physically. It cannot be beaten if it is handled properly.

What comes from the heart is individual feeling. What comes from power is authority to back itself up in whatever way it likes because it is like a thousand hearts beating as one. If power is used the correct way it can never be beaten.

Andrew

Lotte Moos said "Oppressive power wants everything to be mechanical." I agree because if the oppressive power cannot control the people they'll lose power. If things are not run smooth things will be questioned. Ireland is a place where oppressive power wants things smooth — by smooth I mean orderly — but look at the IRA: every chance they get they try to get oppressive power out. Even in Roman times oppressive power wanted things mechanical but the son of God spread the word of God, didn't he? — and to make things smooth and mechanical he was killed. The same thing applies in South Africa today. The point she is making is quite true in my mind.

Kevin A

THE ANIMALS TRY TO WIN ORPHEUS BACK IN THE END.

There was talk of loyalty to others. This could apply to animals. When they ran into the forest to hide they may have been thinking of themselves but then they remembered that it was Orpheus who had previously calmed them with his music, that it was Orpheus who had brought them closer together not only in distance but in unison. Perhaps they felt an obligation to Orpheus to soothe him from his troubles.

Gary

FABLE.

A fable is meant as a way of telling to explain a point as clearly as it may be so the ending cannot be changed because it was meant to be in that form and no different. It can only differ if it is for a different meaning — in that case it is a different fable.

Errol

I AM NOT A PROFESSIONAL WRITER. I ONLY WRITE AT NIGHT.

I do not agree with everything I read. I hate reading a story and not liking the finish. I am not a professional writer but I do my homework at night. Lotte Moos heard us reading our work out and she liked it. I also like the work of IV/C especially mine although Mustafa should have read his story. I also thought Kevin Soobadoo's was good.

Nicholas F

I think she is saying "I write to please myself; if others like it, good but really it's for me." Professional writers write for money and will do a quick piece just for money.

Kevin A

I think she·meant that to be a professional writer one must make it a full-time occupation, meaning writing in the daytime as well. I think also that when you write at night the thoughts that come into your mind are not really vivid — the start of a dream, maybe; to gain merit as a professional writer the work must be done with clear vision.

Andrew

YOU NEVER KNOW HOW A STORY WILL FINISH.

This I believe is true because she starts writing with an idea and builds on it, putting into it more and more of her own emotions, feelings and the views held at the time.

Gary

It is right what she said about the ending of a story. I myself never reach the end of a story until my mind has either nothing left on the matter or I am sure it is the best way to end. I try to get the most out of my head and I have an idea off another idea. What she is saying is that she writes until it is appropriate [to stop]. But what I think is that nobody ever has the ending because it never ends; there is only a cut in the episode which can be followed on by the next chapter.

Errol

Take that last quotation from the writing of an obscure 4/C boy in an obscure London comprehensive school classroom. Is the substance of it so very different in its import from the following items taken from the work of much more notable thinkers?

The story is always *out there* but the important step has to be taken. The unremitting flow of events must first be selectively attended to, interpreted as holding relationships, causes, motives, feelings, consequences — in a word, *meanings*. To give an order to this otherwise unmanageable flux we must take another step and invent, yes, invent beginnings and endings for out there are no such things. Even so stark an ending as death is only an ending when we have made a story out of life.

Harold Rosen, from *Stories and Meanings*

I am producing too many stories at once because what I want is for you to feel, around the story, a saturation of other stories that I could tell or maybe will tell or who knows may have already told on some other occasion, a space full of stories that perhaps is simply my lifetime, where you can move in all directions, as in space, always finding stories that cannot be told until other stories are told first.

Italo Calvino, from *If on a winter's night a traveller*

Myth is circular; it always starts again.

Lotte Moos

[*Narratives*] stop nowhere, and the exquisite problem of the artist is eternally to draw, by a geometry of his own, the circle in which they shall *appear* to do so.

Henry James, from his preface to *Roderick Hudson*

Errol is not expressing their ideas, or mine, or anyone else's but his own. They have emerged, like those of his classmates, as a result of his own experience of making stories allied to real-life contact with other storymakers, such as Lotte — and his own peers.

This is not a book about narratology or about literary criticism or even about recording speculation and rationalization. And yet all these final excerpts from 4/C's writings contain those elements, and all grew out of the told story. Again, all levels of ability have been represented. Some pupils, like Errol, move into the world of high thinkers; they struggle, though not always successfully, to formulate their own theory concerning the nature of power, of human feeling, of the writer's task. Some need to make abstract statements; others negotiate more easily through the here and now of their own lives or through recollections in tranquillity. Some relate their ideas to international events of the moment; others can look back into history to find their proofs. Some just make it all up. One speaks with a solemn tongue; another, like Nicholas, cannot omit a giggle. Every boy has something to say: the door must be open for each different voice so that all can benefit from the proceeds. We are all storytellers.

Fourteen

A BACKWARD GLANCE

■ ANOTHER SHOSHANA STORY

Once there was a little girl. It was morning and she found another little girl her age. They went into one little girl's house that woke up this morning. And then they went out to play. And then they played together.

And one said, "Where are we going to play?"

And the other said, "In the sand box."

And the other said, "Oh!" And the same one said, "Alright."

And the other one said, "Goodnight." And one little girl spent the night at the other little girl's house.

[*Grandma lost a sentence at this point*]

And they were friends together.

And they never did terrible things together.

And none of it was nonsense.

And they made a thing together and made friendship and they also made peace.

And they put their hands up and they sang a song. They sang "Twinkle Twinkle." They became little sisters and they said, "Mommy, mommy." And they sang, "Twinkle, Twinkle Little Star . . ."

[*She sings the whole song*]

> *Twinkle, twinkle little star,*
> *How I wonder what you are!*
> *Up above the world so high,*
> *Like a diamond in the sky . . .*
> Little Star ends it. The end.

I was right about Shoshana. That tale came through our letter box several weeks after I had said my bold say in chapter nine about the kind of stories Shoshana would compose. It seems that she is indeed an inventor inveterate of happy stories. This one is more so than the first. Here her joy spills out still further: "And they also made peace." Orpheus-like, they sing, these little sisters under the skin, to mommy and to the firmament.

I wonder what Shoshana looks like. I wonder if she looks like the sort of person who would make up happy stories. She may well do. On the other hand, her stories are but inventions — there's always the chance that when Grandma Goodman's not about, she and her friend do in fact get up to "terrible things together," and who knows what that might possibly mean? The mind boggles . . .

But if there are all sorts of children together, having a range of skills, cultures, backgrounds, origins, languages, dialects, perceptions, experiences, fears, hopes, aspirations, joys . . . then the possibilities for exciting interactions over a story are as infinite as the stars that twinkle alongside Kevin Als's time-wrapped starship.

That's how it was with the children I taught. They made rich stories. And while making those stories together, they made friendships. And they also made peace. And none of it was nonsense.

This is Shoshana.

STORIES OF STORIES

A POSTSCRIPT BY HAROLD ROSEN

I come from a family of cloth feelers. They were all in tailoring: pressers, cutters, felling hands, buttonhole makers, machinists. My grandfather was a machinist. More than half a century curved over a sewing machine had shaped him, as anyone looking at his back could have told you. Give him a snippet of cloth and he would raise it to his nose and take a noisy sniff. Then he'd feel it. First he'd pick it up between his finger and thumb and go snap. Then he'd stroke it slowly with the flat of his hand, and finally take up the piece and crumple it tightly, then suddenly let it go. At the end he might say, "You could make a good suit out of that."

You can't do the same thing with a book. You can't feel it for other readers and pronounce upon it. I want to do something different. This book emerges from and presents an interlocking set of classroom events that revolve around narratives — storytelling and retelling, story writing. The narratives stand on their own feet and you could, if you felt so disposed, read them on their own as you might any collection of stories. But then you would miss the accounts of how they were woven into the life of classrooms and how, collectively, they are the autobiography of a teacher.

For this book is more than a description of classroom practices centred around narratives. It is a demonstration of the uncanny power of narrative as a means of presenting, analyzing and weighing experiences, the teacher's experiences of using narrative as a focus of classroom practice. It is an autobiographical story of stories. It is one long metanarrative — the name which has been given to all those features of a story which refer to the story itself. In Todorov's words, "every story relates across the plot of events, the story of its own creation, of its own story." This book reminds us of the familiar, "Did you hear the one about . . .?" Stories about stories are commoner than we think. And like all stories, we learn from them.

It would have been possible, of course, to have presented the experiences in this book in a quite different, but recognized, fashion, like the way I was taught to write up chemistry experiments. It would have emerged as a neat set of lesson plans, with a smooth description of the procedures and the results. But since the point of the book is that stories are a means of knowing and of communicating that knowing, its writer had to show confidence in that conviction by saying, by implication, to her readers, "I will tell you the stories of the stories. If I do the job well, you will learn from them, from the very fabric of their telling and from my attempt to give coherence to the hurly-burly of a teacher's daily encounters." For narrative is nothing if not a supreme means of rendering otherwise chaotic, shapeless events into a coherent whole, saturated with meaning. And isn't that what teachers do between the speeches and lectures at conferences and courses?

For a number of years I have been chasing the huge literature that has accummulated around narrative, and looking at narrative in the classroom. I've learned many things in the process. As I consumed scholarly books, research papers and articles, and grappled with complex theories of narrative, I became increasingly aware that as yet no major work has appeared which presents a coherent educational theory of narrative. Even more significant, perhaps, we have no full accounts of narrative in the classroom by teachers who believe in it as a pillar of the curriculum and who have translated that belief into practice — the educational world doesn't accept that telling the tales of teaching as richly and honestly as we know how is a totally valid means of teaching each other.

I seize avidly upon books which are, if you like, autobiographical novels of classroom life. I think gratefully of masterpieces like Makarenko's *Road to Life*, Sylvia Ashton Warner's *Spinster*, and some of the early writings of A.S. Neil, like *A Dominie's Log*. There are no neat recipes in those books. An American teacher, Valerie Polakow, one of the few who believe that teachers' stories are a valid kind of research, writes:

In every story there exists a dialectic between teller and listener and at some moment the horizons of telling and listening fuse . . . and as our lived worlds merge, engagement begets reciprocity and participation in the world of the other and evokes from us the call to act. The educator/researcher as storyteller is a metaphor for engagement, a call to action.

Which is why this book is not a program. The stories of the boys of this school, embedded as they are in the stories of their teacher, are an importunate invitation to every other teacher, a call to action. In Abit's story, for example, in chapter three, the nuances of possible action, especially in multi-lingual settings, are there for all to see.

It is, then, the double articulation of this book that makes it a particular kind of learning instrument for teachers. For they will see both the intensely specific features in one Tottenham school and one teacher's journey, and also what can be generalized, adapted and made newly specific. Different stories will be composed by other teachers and students. I do not look at and enjoy my friends' gardens to make a replica of them in my own, but I learn from every one of them.

The point is made, except that we are surrounded by the hum of powerful voices — around the globe — saying something quite different. What I read in North America seems like a conscious paraphrase of some official pronouncement from Britain, and vice versa. The cry everywhere is for precise, testable outcomes for all curricular practices, tied to specific ages or grades.

Just look back at the story of Orpheus and Eurydice in chapter eleven, and at the intricate and varied responses of the boys. They were deeply moved, and who could doubt that there would be both long-lasting and ephemeral effects upon them. But try to list testable outcomes of the telling of that story! Which is not to say that we could not check how well they could recall it, or whether they had mastered its "story grammar."

I want to show that the narrative mode of this book is not just one teacher's fancy, but that it has standing behind it a whole universe of scholarly thought. Sadly, this wealth of ideas has scarcely touched mainstream educational thinking. I point to this intellectual hinterland not simply to lend respectability to the endeavours of one classroom teacher (not to be sneezed at in these contentious times!), but to buttress her descriptions and stories with impeccable credentials, to demonstrate that, as is often the case, what is done partly intuitively through the devious and untraceable paths of experience and reflection has standing behind it the most powerful theoretical support. It has in fact much greater support than many of the language practices currently being urged upon us.

If you start out, as I did, to explore what has been written about narrative, you will soon discover that there is a lot more of it than you had ever imagined. There is no discipline in the social sciences and humanistic studies which has not turned its attention to it. Anthropologists know that to understand a culture they must not only know its stories, but focus on who tells them, when and how. Dell Hymes has devoted a whole work to the subject: *In vain I tried to tell you.* In literary studies, attention has shifted from the evaluation of canonical novels (the "great books") to how narrative works in novels and short stories, from the "simplest" folktale to the modernist anti-novel. Back in the 60's, Roland Barthes showed how all narratives have a complex structure and, with dazzling virtuosity, went on to demonstrate in his book *S/Z* that a story by Balzac wove together its meaning through the working of different codes. Discourse analysts like Deborah Tannen and Livia Polanyi have revealed for us the subtleties of everyday spontaneous storytelling that crops up unrehearsed in casual conversation. Historians like Hayden White discuss the problems of transmuting their evidence from a recital of discrete facts into a narrative. Theologians now scrutinize the Bible as a narratized text, not simply a devotional work. To penetrate its meanings one must penetrate its narrative methods. Linguists, for so long marooned in sentence structure, realize that to justify their claims as scientists of language they must offer an analysis of narrative. Thus Raguaiya Husan included in her book *Linguistics, language and verbal arts* a chapter analyzing *Necessity's Child* by Angus Wilson. Psychologists with an interest in how we think and learn soon discover that narrative is so universal a resource that they need to study it to understand its meaning for the human psyche. Therapy has entered popular consciousness sufficiently for us to be aware that therapists work upon life stories which are told and retold. Folklorists are looking afresh at the printed versions of fairy tales (Grimm, Anderson, Perrault), and Zipes has shown that these were carefully doctored to make them acceptable to middle-class audiences. Ethnographers look at the different ways in which stories are told by different ethnic groups, social classes, age groups and genders. Shirley Brice Heath, in *Ways With Words*, meticulously analyzes the differences between black and white working-class communities and shows the consequences in the classroom of different storytelling styles. Richard Bauman, in *Story, Performance and Event*, shows how the transcribed texts of oral storytellers never do justice to them as performers — the very point made in chapter six of this book where the writer discovers to her dismay that the text of her told story is a damp, limp thing compared with the tape.

This already lengthy recital is far from exhaustive, but enough, I hope, to signpost the ferment of interest which in the last decade or so has surrounded narrative. And alongside these works, we have had a revival of oral storytelling, even whole festivals of it. The storyteller is back in the marketplace, luring folk from their TV sets and stereos just when we had been told that storytelling was dead, slaughtered by commercial culture. A few months ago I sat in an audience listening to a group of Caribbean storytellers, all very different in narrative style, and at one point I was moved to turn round in my seat and look at the sophisticated, mostly adult London audience. Their jaws were dropping and their eyes intently focused — like any bunch of primary school kids who have listened to my stories.

I keep wondering what is happening and why. Why, at this very moment, do we find both the great scholars and a classroom teacher like Betty Rosen writing books on narrative? For that matter, why does it turn out that what I thought was my own purely personal interest is in fact a tiny pulse in a world shift of activity? I know of no attempt to explain this burgeoning interest. The answer may lie in the fact that we live in a world cowering under terrifying dehumanizing forces that make ordinary people feel puny and helpless, and thus easily manipulated — that give them very limited powers of reflection and creativity. It may be more than ever necessary to seek out and cherish those universal human activities that display inventiveness, cunning evasion of oppression and communicative ruses of all kinds. For everyone is a storyteller and, given some nurturing, can become a better one. This book makes us see again and again that, once set loose, the storytelling impulse enables the most unlikely people to deploy unsuspected linguistic resources and strategies.

Whatever the reason for so many recently published books finding their way onto my shelves, this new abundance of theory and analysis is founded on certain axiomatic propositions. As Hayden says:

. . . far from being one code among many that a culture may utilize for endowing experience with meaning, narrative is a metacode, a human universal . . .
Arising, as Barthes says, between our experience of the world and our efforts to describe that experience in language, narrative "ceaselessly substitutes meaning for a straightforward copy of the events recounted." And it would follow that, on this view, the absence of narrative capacity or a refusal of narrative indicates an absence or refusal of meaning itself.

We have been so mesmerized by the intellectual culture of our times, so intimidated by spurious claims for the superiority of what has come to be called "expository discourse," that we are frequently disposed to be apologetic about narrative. There are contexts in which the dismissive word "anecdote" is used to brush aside the most sensitive and perceptive comment, while pedestrian and often empty abstract propositions are treated with respect.

We should militantly assert that the students in this book are meaning-makers even when — perhaps especially when — they are retelling. They rework the stories they have heard to make new meanings, to shift their view of the world or amplify it. At the same time, they are constructing their own social selves, as Wayne Booth suggests:

Who I am *now* is best shown by the stories I can tell and who I am to become is best determined by the stories I can *learn* to tell.

For there is learning to be done and the evidence accumulated in these pages shows that the impulse to narrative is already present in every student, and that a storytelling culture in the classroom refines and enlarges upon that impulse. The students undoubtedly already knew how to begin and end stories, but, as we see in chapter twelve, new and exciting possibilities emerged as they were encouraged to reflect upon alternative strategies.

Wherever we turn in the literature, sooner or later we stumble upon the results of sustained study encapsulated in a phrase. Narrative, they tell us, is:

- the central function or instance of the human mind (Frederic Jamison);
- a primary cognitive instrument making the flux of experience comprehensible (Richard Bauman);
- a primary act of mind (Barbara Hardy).

Bauman's recent book analyzes Texan oral narratives. He concludes:

When one looks to the social practices by which social life is accomplished one finds — with surprising frequency — people telling stories to each other as a means of giving cognitive and emotional coherence to experience, constructing and negotiating social identity . . . investing the experimental landscape with moral significance.

Teachers launching themselves and their students (of any age) into storytelling should be encouraged by words like these. For how much of the curriculum can lay claim to the simultaneous interlocking of cognitive, emotional, social and moral involvement? What is more, these statements are not being made about great works of fiction, which are conventionally accepted as having an unchallenged place somewhere in the curriculum, but about the human disposition to narratize experience. This suggests that narrative in school is not something to be *consumed* (in written form) but something to be *made* by every person in every possible way, and that it is limitless in its possibilities.

I want to recall Jerome Bruner's work. His reputation stands high not only in the world of academic psychology but also in education, because he has always been ready to address practical teaching matters and to apply his theory and research to the curriculum. Like Vygotsky, whom he admires, he has for many years investigated the relationship between language and thought. I might have guessed that sooner or later he would turn his attention to narrative and have something to say about narrative and thinking. It turns out that he has for a long time been a leading participant in seminars on narrative theory and practice at the New School for Social Research in New York. And in his most recent book, *Actual*

Minds, Possible Worlds, I found a bold and provocative attempt to assess narrative. I'll attempt to give the essence of his ideas.

Brunner sets out to show that narrative is not simply one option among many when we speak or write, that it is, rather, one of two fundamental possibilities:

There are two modes of cognitive functioning, two modes of thought, each providing distinctive ways of ordering experience, of constructing reality. The two (though complementary) are irreducible to one another. Efforts to ignore one at the expense of the other inevitably fail to capture the rich diversity of human thought.

Once again the key idea is "ways of ordering experience," and one of Bruner's two modes is, indeed, narrative. The other he calls "paradigmatic": the mode we would most readily recognize in its logico-scientific form, the kind of thinking which needs no advocates in schools. We may never encounter logico-scientific thought, but inevitably we will perceive the world narratively, handle experience by composing it into stories. The Tottenham boys in this book will not have had much more than a brush with logico-scientific thought, but every citation shows them to be steeped in the ways of narrative thought.

Bruner tells us that the paradigmatic mode works through:

. . . categorization or conceptualization and the operations by which categories are established, instantiated, idealized and related to one another to form a system.

By contrast, narrative works by constructing simultaneously two landscapes:

. . . the landscape of action, where the constituents are the arguments of action: agent, intention or goal, situation, instrument, something corresponding to a "story grammar"

and

. . . the landscape of consciousness; what those involved in the action know, think and feel, or do not know, think and feel.

I have done no more than give you Bruner's starting points which he elaborates with great verve. No summary would do his ideas justice. Although he begins by speaking of all narrative, he very rapidly narrows his attention to written fiction of accepted reputation, as though the stories you and I tell each other are not worthy of his attention. All the same, his claim stands: narrative is one of the two branches of human thought. There are some other remarks he makes which might serve as a gloss on the stories in this book:

> One gets a sense of the psychology of genre by listening to readers "tell back" a story they have just read or spontaneously "tell" a story about a happening in their lives. Genre seems to be a way of both organizing the structure of events and organizing the telling of them — a way that can be used for one's own storytelling, or, indeed, for placing the stories one is reading or hearing.

As we grow in our narrative resources we come to recognize and compose stories which follow different sets of conventions. Very early, children can recognize and produce the telltale signs of a fairy tale. Later they will do the same for science fiction, an historical episode, an anecdote of personal experience and so on. All stories feed greedily on other stories. We can easily detect in the retellings in this book the sense of genre which, put quite simply, means knowing how to compose a particular kind of story. We can go even farther than Bruner and say that, given the liberating encouragement of the teacher, retelling can be a profoundly creative activity. Lotte Moos's Orpheus story in chapter thirteen reveals the daring leaps a reteller can make. For stories do not offer single meanings. They form interlocking sets of meanings, and listening to a story is a search for these meanings through the meanings we already possess. In retelling, we both repeat the words of others and change them. Even our own personal stories we change in new contexts, carrying forward some of the old, but shifting, however slightly, the meanings of the story. We are incorrigible reworkers of our own and other people's stories.

It is worth lingering on this point. We have come to believe that creativity in language consists in the production of novel text as distinct from the reproduction of existing text. What higher praise can we offer than to say that a story is original? A reading of this book will show how superficial that view is. It runs counter to all we know about the history of storytelling and all we know about narrative practices. In composing their retellings, these boys were doing the same as little children do when they retell their favourite stories — only they have a richer repertoire of resources to draw upon. Therefore, they know how to take all kinds of liberties with the original story. In many schools, as Betty Rosen points out, an invitation to retell can only be construed by the students as an invitation *to get it right*, word-perfect if possible. (Indeed, this tradition haunts Bruner himself when he investigates retelling). Give back exactly what you were given by teacher and textbook — isn't that the dominant peremptory command of the curriculum? That's how you get good marks, isn't it?

But examine carefully the bold liberty-takers in this book. They elaborate, compress, innovate, discard. Not one of them is a mindless mimic. They act as all good storytellers do: they take what they want, shift nuances, maybe turn the whole story upside down. These changes repay study, for they reveal the creativity of retelling and the delicate tension between reproduction and invention. Traditional storytellers were never mere echoes, but creative performers, putting their personal stamp on traditional tales.

We can see a narrative alchemy at work here, one we all need to understand more fully. Paradoxically, the fact that the story is already given liberates the reteller from certain basic burdens of invention and frees the imagination to play inventively with what is available. So we see the boys giving their own inflection to a story, as their teacher did in telling it. The creative judgement of the storyteller is always at work busily bending it to his purposes. Betty Rosen shows us that the teacher has a unique role here: to emancipate her students from the stultifying demand for recall, to set them free to take over a story and bend it to their own intentions, as a little Bangladeshi girl did who took a story I told and changed the protaganist from a resourceful young man to an even more resourceful young woman. De Certeau, who believes that everyday stories constitute a major means by which ordinary people evade dominant and oppressive meanings in society, remarks:

The significance of a story that is well-known and therefore classifiable can be reversed by a single "circumstantial" detail . . . "The insignificant detail" inserted into the framework that supports it makes the commonplace produce other effects.

Enough is enough. All that I have read of narratology (as it is now called) points unequivocally in one direction: we need to give greater space to narrative in the curriculum. This book is about storytellers in the *secondary school*, which for some will be a surprise, for others positively outlandish. As children move through typical school systems, spontaneous, student-created narrative is at least marginalized or, more likely, outlawed. Story writing is edged out as other kinds of privileged discourse are installed. Teachers, especially in secondary school, yield too easily to the notion that there is something cognitively inferior about the telling of tales. To give narrative the ample space given by the writer of this book requires the teacherly nerve to stand up to prevailing assumptions.

Easily said! Intellectual life is more and more haunted by a dilemma. On the one hand, it produces powerful propositions, abstractions and principles which offer the seductive possibility of making sense of a chaos of evidence. On the other hand, such a formidable armoury often leaves a sense of dissatisfaction. The sense of the actual, the particular, the idiosyncratic, the taste of direct experience seems to get lost or buried or made to appear irrelevant. This is particularly true when we ourselves are the object of our study. The demand for "case studies" arises from that powerful feeling that there is more to life than generalizations can encompass. We are always greedy for accounts of "actual" experience which give off that special aroma of the authentic. Such accounts are neither a-theoretical nor anti-theoretical, for always, however implicit, there are principles and assumptions at work. So it is with all narratives of personal experience, including narratives of teaching experience. It would be true to say that there is a huge reservoir of innovatory teaching experience which is never drawn on because it is never translated into stories. To know about it, you have to haunt the informal gatherings at conferences and courses, keep your ear to the ground, seek out all those occasions when by word of mouth teachers tell each other their stories. This book turns that oral practice into written text.

A final word. Teaching and learning never change without a special kind of imaginative act, which all the curriculum guides in the world cannot render unnecessary. You may be persuaded that it is important to become more conversant with narrative theory. You may be inspired to turn your classroom into one where stories flow and become a major means of learning and developing linguistic powers. But then, you need to translate your enthusiasm into day-to-day practices. How will you make your first move? How do you learn to tell stories? Where will you find them? How, in a phrase, do your principles undergo that amazing metamorphosis into everyday encounters? Only by your own imaginative weighing of your students and their history, and yourself and your history. You must trust your own inventiveness. That is what this book is about.

GLOSSARY

■ THE SCHOOLS

Primary schools:

British children normally begin their primary education when they are five years old, or just before, and transfer to a secondary school at eleven. Many primary schools have all their children on the same site, though sometimes there may be separate buildings housing the "infants," the under-sevens, and the "juniors," the sevens to elevens.

In Clydach, the Infant School was a completely separate building, several hundred metres down the road from the Junior School, each having its own Principal — or Headteacher, as is the term in England and Wales. This is not uncommon in urban areas.

Secondary schools:

There are over four thousand maintained secondary schools in England and Wales at the moment, where pupils are obliged to stay until the age of sixteen, though they may become sixth-formers and remain voluntarily for up to three more years.

Grammar Schools provide a mainly academic course for selected pupils. Secondary Modern Schools provide a more general education for the majority who fail to gain entry to a grammar school on the basis of the 11+ examination — "the scholarship," as we called it at Clydach Junior. This division was the norm in the mid-fifties when I began teaching, but already comprehensivization was underway in the major urban centres, notably London. It was in fact in a Comprehensive School that I did my teaching practice during my one year of post-graduate professional training, leading to my PGCE — Post Graduate Certificate in Education. The aspiration was for comprehensive schools to take in *all* children at the age of eleven. However, they often co-exist with private and selective schools. Leaving aside the matter of age range, the comprehensive school is most like the North American high school.

As a result of comprehensive reorganization, the number of grammar schools in England fell from 1180 to 175 between 1965 and 1984. The decrease in the number of pupils at secondary modern schools over the same period was from 660,000 to 117,187. The reorganization did away with the invidious and largely inefficient 11 examination for the majority of the school population, but the tide is turning again now, and soon there will be tests at 7, 11, 14 and, with the introduction of the new GCSE this year (1987), at 16.

Private schools:
    Roughly seven percent of the total school population in England, and two percent in Wales, attend independent schools that are funded by fees and endowments. They cater to pupils of all ages, and a relatively high proportion provide boarding. They include the Preparatory Schools, for boys and girls from 7 to 13 and over, and the Public Schools. The latter term must be enormously confusing for foreigners, since the name suggests the very opposite from the actuality!

■ BRITISH MULTI-CULTURAL POLICIES

The concept of multi-cultural education has developed over the years as a result of the presence in schools of large numbers of pupils who are linguistically and culturally "different" from the indigenous majority, many of them visually obvious in the classrooms. Successive governments have adopted a variety of assimilationist and/or paternalistic attitudes in this situation. In spite of official European (EEC) dictates to the effect that mother tongues and minority cultures should be fostered within the system, little or no response has come from central government.
    Informed practitioners in the field, many schools, and several local education authorities have formulated their own anti-racist and multi-cultural policies, however. These recognize that bilingualism and multi-culturalism within our schools provide a source of benefit to all, rather than a "problem" to be suffered. At best, whole curricula are designed to put this principle into practice. At worst, the pupil members of minority ethnic groups are expected to set aside their ethnicity and get on with learning how to become as English as possible as fast as possible.

■ NARRATOLOGY

Narratology is a comparatively recent member of the brotherhood of "-ologies" (see the postscript). As it became clear that linguists' structural analyses of language left unanswered many questions to do with *meaning*, the attention turned towards whole texts — literature, in fact. The attempt is to discover the "rules" common to all narrative composition. The misfortune is that even the most intriguing writers in this field look at the works of "great" authors to prove their points. Oral narrative is not, as yet, on the narratologists' "agenda." Perhaps they are scared: it is altogether too human and unruly!

REFERENCES

■ BETTY'S BOOKS

Bayly, Thomas Haynes. "The Mistletoe Bough."

Berger, John. *About Time*. Jonathan Cape, 1985.

Calvino, Italo. *If on a Winter's Night a Traveler*. Harcourt Brace Jovanovich, 1986.

Caribbean Anthology. Inner London Education Authority.

D'Arcy, Pat, ed. *Bonds*. The English Project Stage 3, Ward Lock Educational. (Excerpt originally published by Wildwood House in *Birth Without Violence*.)

Garner, Alan. "Granny Reardun" in *The Stone Book*.

Graves, Robert. *The Greek Myths*, vol. 1, rev. ed. Peng;uin, 1960.

"Greek Myths" in Macdonald's Junior Reference Library.

James, Henry. Preface to *Roderick Hudson*, 1874.

Marshall, Alan. "How I Tell My Stories," from an interview by Norma Ferris. Thomas Nelson (Australia), 1974.

Moos, Lotte."Orpheus and the Bear" in *Time to Be bold*. Centerprise Trust, with the financial assistance of Hackney Writers' Workshop.

Pepper, Dennis, ed. *That Once Was Me*. The English Project, Stage 2, Ward Lock Educational. (Originally published by Penguin, 1973.)

Ransome, Arthur. *Old Peter's Russian Tales*. Jonathan Cape, 1984.

Ransome, Arthur. *Swallowdale*. Jonathan Cape, 1980.

Roach, E.M. "To my Mother" in *Caribbean Verse*, O.R. Dathorne, ed. Heinemann, 1967.

Rosen, Harold. *Stories and Meanings*. NATE, 1985.

Rosen, Michael. "The King Who Promised" in *When Did You Last Wash Your Feet?* Andre Deutsch.

Shakespeare, William. *Henry VIII*.

■ HAROLD'S BOOKS

Ashton-Warner, Sylvia. *Spinster*. Simon and Schuster, 1986.

Barthes, Roland. "Introduction to the Structuralist Analysis of Narrative" in *Barthes: Selected Writings*, S. Sonntag, ed. Fontana, 1982.

Barthes, Roland. *S/Z*. Jonathan Cape, 1976.

Bauman, Richard. *Story, Performance, and Event: Contextual Studies of Oral Narrative*. Cambridge University Press, 1986.

Booth, Wayne. "Narrative as a Mold of Character" in *A Telling Exchange*, report of the 17th Conference of Language in Inner City Schools, University of London Institute of Education, 1983.

Bruner, Jerome. *Actual Minds, Possible Worlds*. Harvard University Press, 1986.

De Certeau, Michel. "On the Oppositional Practices of Everyday Life," in *Social Texts*, vol. 1, 3, Fall, 1980.

Hardy, Barbara. "Towards a Poetic of Fiction: An Approach Through Narrative" in *Novel: A Forum on Fiction*, Brown University, 1968.

Hasan, Ruqaiya. *Linguistics, Language and Verbal Arts*. Deakin University Press, 1985.

Heath, Shirley Brice. *Ways with Words: Language, Life and Work in Communities and Classrooms*. Cambridge University Press, 1983.

Hymes, Dell. *In Vain I Tried to Tell You*. University of Pennsylvania Press, 1981.

Jameson, Frederic. *The Political Unconscious: Narrative as a Socially Symbolic Act*. Cornell University Press, 1981.

Makarenko, A.S. *The Road to Life*. Moscow, Foreign Languages Publishing House.

Neill, A.S. *A Dominie's Log*. H. Jenken, 1915.

Polakow, Valerie. "Whose Stories Should We Tell? A Call to Action," in *Language Arts*, vol. 62, 6, 1985, pages 826-835.

Polanyi, Livia. "Literary Complexity in Everyday Storytelling" in *Spoken and Written Language*, D. Tannen. Ablex, 1982.

Todorov, Tzvetan. *The Poetics of Prose*, translated by Richard Howard. Cornell University Press, 1977.

White, Hayden. "The Value of Narrativity" in *On Narrative*, W.J.T. Mitchell, ed. University of Chicago Press, 1981.

Zipes, Jack. *Fairy Tales and the Art of Subversion*. Methuen, 1985.